11/06

Ka[...]

[...]inking of you
And praying for you!
In His love —
Joe + Debbie

Kaye Litzinger

Joe + Debbie Negley

Tranquility for a Woman's Soul: Simple Thoughts and Scriptures to Calm Your Spirit

Copyright © 2006 by The Zondervan Corporation
ISBN-10: 0-310-80863-4
ISBN-13: 978-0-310-80863-3

Requests for information should be addressed to:
Inspirio, The gift group of Zondervan
Grand Rapids, Michigan 49530

Project Manager: Tom Dean
Design Manager: Jody Langley
Production Management: Matt Nolan
Design: studiogearbox.com

Printed in China
06 07 08 / 4 3 2 1

TRANQUILITY

FOR A

Woman's Soul

STILLNESS IN THE STORM
God's Presence Through Difficult Times

SERENITY OF SPIRIT
Finding a Quiet Place in a Noisy World

PASSING THE PEACE
Giving to Others from the Tranquility in Your Heart

HEALING OF HEAVEN
Tranquility in the Hope of Eternal Life

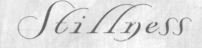
IN THE STORM

GOD'S PRESENCE THROUGH DIFFICULT TIMES

DELIVER ME

*I sought the L*ORD*, and he answered me;*
  he delivered me from all my fears....
*This poor man called, and the L*ORD *heard him;*
  he saved him out of all his troubles....
A righteous man may have many troubles,
  *but the L*ORD *delivers him from them all....*
*The L*ORD *redeems his servants;*
  no one will be condemned who takes refuge in him.

PSALM 34:4, 6, 19, 22

P salm 34 begins with David praising God.
  Fear had filled his heart because of the
trouble he had been experiencing. Knowing and
believing in the power of prayer, he sought the
Lord, his sure source of help.

  God heard and delivered him out of ALL his
fears, ALL his troubles, ALL his afflictions. No
wonder his heart was so full of praise to God!

  Fear! Trouble! Affliction! Who has not
experienced them? Fear has filled our hearts,

troubles have mounted, afflictions have crushed us. What God did for David, he can do for us. If we seek him, he will hear and deliver. He has promised to deliver us from EVERY trouble, from EVERY affliction.

Deliverance may not come in the way we expect it, or at the time we want it. He may not deliver us out of them all, but he will deliver us in the midst of them all.

In his later years of life, George Frederick Handel lost his money. His health failed. His right side became paralyzed. His creditors were threatening him with imprisonment for non-payment of his debts. He had no place to go but to God. Putting his trust completely in him to meet his needs, he decided to go into seclusion. There he spent much time in meditation and prayer. Out of this time spent with God came the greatest of all his oratorios, *The Messiah*.

Someone has said, "He who knows God and remembers that he has a father's heart and a mother's concern for his own, will never be panic-stricken even when all that is considered stable and permanent comes down with a crash."[1]

Millie Stamm

MEDITATIONS ON

God's Deliverance

---

*Do not be afraid. Stand firm and you will see the
deliverance the LORD will bring you today.*

EXODUS 14:13

From the LORD comes deliverance.
    May your blessing be on your people.

PSALM 3:8

The LORD is my rock, my fortress and my deliverer;
    my God is my rock, in whom I take refuge.
    He is my shield and the horn of my salvation,
        my stronghold.

PSALM 18:2

*[God] has delivered us from such a deadly peril, and he
will deliver us. On him we have set our hope that he will
continue to deliver us.*

2 CORINTHIANS 1:10

You, O LORD, have delivered my soul from death,
    my eyes from tears,
    my feet from stumbling,
that I may walk before the LORD
    in the land of the living.

PSALM 116:8–9

A Refuge and a
Hiding Place

A young woman simply decided to lock herself in her bedroom one day. She wouldn't come out for anything—not for crying babies or a questioning husband. She was disappointed with her life and depressed about what seemed to be a bleak future. She just wanted to hide. Can you relate?

Most of us ignore [the need to hide away] until life grows overwhelming and hiding out turns into a traumatic, last-ditch attempt to save our sanity. Then the baby screams louder, the toddler bangs on the door harder, the confused husband turns angry, and we feel guilty. Shouldn't we be able to keep up, to continue [on] as long as everybody needs us? If we feel like hiding, aren't we weak-willed or irresponsible?

No. To feel like hiding is to be human, to recognize the soul's desire to pull away and within, to respond to a need for replenishment. The problem is, we don't hide often enough. If we practiced a periodic hiding, a repeated running away to God—often just for moments, sometimes for hours or days—we'd be less susceptible to letting the daily grind pulverize us.

The Lord doesn't shame us or chastise us for wanting to hide. He says, "Come to me. I will nurture and fill you. When you lock away with me, for a brief time the world will go away. I am the rock, your hiding place."[2]

Judith Couchman

Hide me, O my Savior, hide me
In Thy holy place;
Resting there beneath Thy glory,
O let me see Thy face.

Hide me, hide me,
O blessed Savior, hide me;
O Savior, keep me,
Safely, O Lord, with Thee.

Hide me, when the storm is raging
O'er life's troubled sea;
Like a dove on ocean's billows,
O let me fly to Thee.

Hide me, when my heart is breaking
With its weight of woe;
When in tears I seek the comfort
Thou canst alone bestow.

Fanny Crosby

MEDITATIONS ON
a Refuge and a Hiding Place

———

Keep me as the apple of your eye [O LORD];
hide me in the shadow of your wings.

PSALM 17:8

In the day of trouble
[the Lord] will keep me safe in his dwelling;
he will hide me in the shelter of his tabernacle
and set me high upon a rock.

PSALM 27:5

You [LORD]; are my hiding place
you will protect me from trouble
and surround me with songs of deliverance.

PSALM 32:7

Rescue me from my enemies, O LORD,
for I hide myself in you.

PSALM 143:9

Let all who take refuge in you [LORD]; be glad,
let them ever sing for joy.
Spread your protection over them,
that those who love your name may rejoice in you.

PSALM 5:11

Though the
Earth Give Way

When everything in our lives and experience is shaken that can be shaken, and only that which cannot be shaken remains, we see that God only is our rock and our foundation, and we learn to have our expectation from him alone.

Psalm 46:2–5 reads,

"Therefore we will not fear, though the earth be removed, and though the mountains be carried into the midst of the sea;

Though the waters thereof roar and be troubled, though the mountains shake with the swelling thereof.

There is a river, the streams whereof shall make glad the city of God. ...

God is in the midst of her; she shall not be moved: God shall help her, and that right early" (KJV).

"Shall not be moved"—what an inspiring declaration! Can we, who are so easily moved by the things of earth, arrive at a place where nothing can upset our temper or disturb our calm? Yes.

The apostle Paul knew it. Everything in Paul's life and experience that could be shaken had been shaken, and he no longer counted his life, or any of life's possessions, dear to him. And we, if we will let God have his way with us, may come to the same place so that neither the little things of life, nor its great and heavy trials, can have power to move us from the peace that passes all understanding, which is the portion of those who rest only on God.

Our souls long for that kingdom that cannot be moved. And this kingdom may be our home, if we will submit to the shakings of God and learn to rest only and always on him.[3]

Hannah Whitall Smith

Though the Earth Give Way

I have set the LORD always before me.
*   Because he is at my right hand,*
*   I will not be shaken.*

PSALM 16:8

When the storm has swept by, the wicked are gone,
*   but the righteous stand firm forever.*

PROVERBS 10:25

[The LORD] alone is my rock and my salvation;
*   he is my fortress, I will never be shaken.*

PSALM 62:2

God's solid foundation stands firm.

2 TIMOTHY 2:19

Hope for the
Sunshine Tomorrow

A friend pours out her troubles to me and
asks, "Should I have hope for this situation? Should I believe God will change things?
Or am I in denial?" These days, soul searchers
probably ask these questions frequently. We've
heard so much about denial and dysfunction, we
can confuse them with biblical faith and hope.

I think my friend expresses a true biblical
hope, because she's doing her part in the situation but [she is] still seeking God as her source
for this need. If she were in denial, she'd stick her
head in the proverbial sand, do nothing, and still
expect God to weave miracles. God is so merci-
ful, he can pull us out of our screwups, but even
the "spiritual greats" advise us to work as if
everything depends on us and pray as if everything depends on God. When we make a choice,
based on God's promises, to abandon ourselves
to him and trustingly throw ourselves into difficult circumstances, hope springs forth and
grows the soul. In ourselves and in those we
encounter.

"Most people want to know if God really makes a difference," explained Rebecca Manley Pippert in *Hope Has Its Reasons*. "Can Jesus help them grow and give meaning and purpose and guidance and strength to their lives too? And when our answer is yes, we have experienced firsthand his power in the midst of pain—we give others hope."

Again, living hopefully, in a biblical sense, traces back to character development—understanding God's desires, and being who he calls us to be. And God asks us to base our being and doing on hope. The hope of his promises, the hope of his return, the hope of heaven.

God, make me a hope-filled person—someone who instills your hope in others. I want to be filled with your heavenly hope and "sure of what I hope for and certain of what I do not see." God, do not let that hope disappoint me.[4]

Judith Couchman

Hoping for the Sunshine Tomorrow

Hope does not disappoint us, because God has poured out his love into our hearts by the Holy Spirit, whom he has given us.

ROMANS 5:5

Weeping may remain for a night,
but rejoicing comes in the morning.

PSALM 30:5

Hope that is seen is no hope at all. Who hopes for what he already has? But if we hope for what we do not yet have, we wait for it patiently.

ROMANS 8:24–25

As for me, I will always have hope;
I will praise you more and more.

PSALM 71:14

STRENGTH IN THE SHADOW

One afternoon, while pounding five-foot iron stakes with a 20-pound mallet in 92-degree heat, in order to anchor the tender fruit trees with rubber hoses against the bending west wind, I noticed I was unusually tired. *It has been a long year*, I thought, then hurried to finish a chapter in a book I was writing. I napped instead and woke feeling feverish. A blood test later revealed that I had developed a case of mononucleosis, which lasts for six weeks—if you're lucky. To bed again. I had endured work-stoppage that fall with grace. The illness of my father had tested my faith in the indomitable goodness of the Lord's will. I had looked on my mother's pain with hope for ease. The petty aggravation of broken things—equipment and bodies— had raised a slight spirit of anger; but this, this was the last straw, and my spirit the camel's back. Days were spent on that pillow, head weighing a ton, fever stopping and starting, as I fought despairing whys. I felt like a child who had been spanked again and again for some unknown error. I was willing to change my unruly behavior but I didn't know what I was doing wrong.

One afternoon Mother came with food. The last thing she needed was to care for me. "Do you have this awful feeling that someone somewhere doesn't like us?" I ventured timidly, afraid to reveal my stricken feelings.

"No," she replied softly. "I have a feeling that Someone somewhere knows we won't be the people he wants us to be without pain. Don't ask where God's love is. This is his shadow side. It is here in these bad things." Laying her hands on me, she prayed for healing. My chastened soul found comfort and the wounds began to mend.

It is wonderful to find a natural mother who can give spiritual grace in the midst of her own trials. Yet I discovered I was also part of a larger inheritance. For one year I was dependent on my joint-heirs in the Kingdom, on my "extended family" of God. They have turned to me hands of mercy and aid and helps.

This is the larger part of my rich and goodly inheritance, this fellowship of suffering and delight, this place of belonging in a homeless world.[5]

Karen Burton Mains

Strength in the Shadow

Even though I walk
   through the valley of the shadow of death,
I will fear no evil,
   for you are with me;
your rod and your staff,
   they comfort me.

PSALM 23:4

Because you [LORD] are my help,
   I sing in the shadow of your wings.
My soul clings to you;
   your right hand upholds me.

PSALM 63:7–8

The people walking in darkness
   have seen a great light;
on those living in the land of the shadow of death
   a light has dawned.

ISAIAH 9:2

They cried to the LORD in their trouble,
   and he saved them from their distress.
He brought them out of darkness and the deepest gloom
   and broke away their chains.

PSALM 107:13–14

My Place of Shelter

The comfort or discomfort of our outward lives depends more largely upon the dwelling place of our bodies than upon almost any other material thing; likewise, the comfort or discomfort of our inward life depends upon the dwelling place of our souls.

Our souls need a comfortable dwelling place, a comfort-filled home, even more than our bodies. When the Lord declares that he has been our dwelling place in all generations, the question remains, Are we living in our dwelling place? Our souls are made for God. He is our natural home, and we can never be at rest anywhere else.

When we read that God, who is our dwelling place, is also our fortress, it can mean only one thing, that if we will live in our dwelling place, we shall be safe and secure from every assault of every enemy that can attack us.

"For in the time of trouble
He shall hide me in His pavilion;
In the secret place of His tabernacle
He shall hide me; He shall set me high upon a rock" (Psalm 27:5 NKJV).

We who are in this dwelling place shall be afraid of nothing; not for the terror by night, nor the arrow by day, nor for the pestilence that hides in the darkness; thousands shall fall beside us and around us, but no evil shall befall the soul that is hidden in this divine dwelling place.

He who cares for the sparrows, and numbers the hairs of our head, cannot possibly fail us. He is an impregnable fortress. The moment I have really committed anything into this divine dwelling place, that moment all fear and anxiety should cease. While I keep anything in my own care, I may well fear and tremble, for it is indeed to the last degree unsafe; but in God's care, no security could be more absolute.[6]

Hannah Whitall Smith

My Place of Shelter

He who dwells in the shelter of the Most High
  will rest in the shadow of the Almighty.
I will say of the LORD, "He is my refuge and my fortress,
  my God, in whom I trust."
Surely he will save you from the fowler's snare
  and from the deadly pestilence.
He will cover you with his feathers,
  and under his wings you will find refuge;
  his faithfulness will be your shield and rampart.
You will not fear the terror of night,
  nor the arrow that flies by day,
nor the pestilence that stalks in the darkness,
  nor the plague that destroys at midday.
A thousand may fall at your side,
  ten thousand at your right hand,
  but it will not come near you.
You will only observe with your eyes
  and see the punishment of the wicked.
If you make the Most High your dwelling—
  even the LORD, who is my refuge—
then no harm will befall you,
  no disaster will come near your tent.
For he will command his angels concerning you
  to guard you in all your ways;
they will lift you up in their hands,
  so that you will not strike your foot against a stone.

PSALM 91:1–12

No Storm Can
Separate Us

When I was a little girl, every Thursday night I went to choir practice with my mother. The director allowed me to sit next to Mother and encouraged me to sing along.

I beamed with pride. My mother was the best soloist in the choir! I leaned against her and tried to make my voice sound like hers, but almost always mine squeaked on the high notes she hit so clearly.

Mother held the music and turned the pages. When I got lost, she pointed to the right note. I didn't understand all the words or know how to read the notes, but I have no doubt that my love for music, and for the Lord, was nurtured through those weekly choir rehearsals.

Tonight I picked Mother up at her apartment and took her to choir with me. Her voice is no longer strong. It cracks on the high notes and slides off key. She isn't asked to sing solos anymore.

Mother's hands get tired holding the music. She forgets to turn the pages and loses her place. I ask her if she wants to look on with me. She nods her head yes.

I think about the doctor's prognosis. Mother isn't that old, but she has an illness similar to Alzheimer's. She is not going to get better, and it's only a matter of time—no one knows how long—before she gets worse.

Suddenly my thoughts are interrupted by the words we're singing. I feel God's presence. He reminds me that even though we grow old and weary, he never changes. He never stops loving us. He will always be with us.

I glance at Mother. She may no longer be able to understand the words she's trying to sing, but I know his Spirit is touching hers. He will allow neither death nor life to separate her from his love.

Thank you, Father, for your promises and for the many ways you gently reassure me that you are with me. Amen.[7]

Marlene Bagnull

MEDITATIONS ON

No Storm Can Separate Us

---

*Who shall separate us from the love of Christ? Shall
trouble or hardship or persecution or famine or naked-
ness or danger or sword? ...*

*No, in all these things we are more than conquerors
through him who loved us. For I am convinced that
neither death nor life, neither angels nor demons, neither
the present nor the future, nor any powers, neither
height nor depth, nor anything else in all creation, will
be able to separate us from the love of God that is in
Christ Jesus our Lord.*

ROMANS 8:35, 37–39

"Even to your old age and gray hairs
    I am he, I am he who will sustain you.
I have made you and I will carry you;
    I will sustain you and I will rescue you,"
[says the LORD*].*

ISAIAH 46:4

*[Jesus said,] "Surely I am with you always,
to the very end of the age."*

MATTHEW 28:20

Hidden Springs

Most trees get their life through the sap that flows up the tree just under the bark. Not so with the palm tree. Its sap flows up the center of the tree, producing new life from the heart of the tree.

The life of the Christian comes from the life of Christ implanted in the heart. "That Christ may dwell in your hearts by faith" (Ephesians 3:17 KJV).

We discover the palm tree not only grows but flourishes in the most unlikely places. Why? Because it has a hidden source of nourishment. Although no water may be visible, the tree sends down a large tap root with other roots deep into the earth, appropriating nourishment from the soil and searching out hidden springs of water.

We have hidden springs of Living Water from which we can draw nourishment. Jesus said, "If anyone is thirsty, let him come to me and drink. For the Scriptures declare that rivers of living water shall flow from the inmost being of anyone who believes in me." (John 7:37–39 TLB) (He was speaking of the Holy Spirit, who would be given to everyone believing in him.)"

The palm tree can withstand winds and hurricanes better than any other tree, not because of greater resistance, but because they bend and yield. When the winds and storms beat upon our lives, we, too, can withstand their fury, as we bend and yield, submissive to God, allowing him to bring good into our lives from them.

Many lives have been saved by finding water near the palm trees. God wants your life and mine to be the means of bringing others to the Water of Life.

When our lives are nourished at his hidden springs, they can flourish like the palm tree, displaying his beauty and uprightness. We will be able to live victoriously above our circumstances.[8]

Millie Stamm

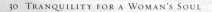

MEDITATIONS ON

Hidden Springs

———

[Jesus said,] "Whoever drinks the water I give him will never thirst. Indeed, the water I give him will become in him a spring of water welling up to eternal life."

JOHN 4:14

He who has compassion on them will guide them
and lead them beside springs of water.

ISAIAH 49:10

"I will make rivers flow on barren heights,
and springs within the valleys.
I will turn the desert into pools of water,
and the parched ground into springs," [says the LORD].

ISAIAH 41:18

[Jesus said,] "I am the Alpha and the Omega,
the Beginning and the End. To him who is thirsty
I will give to drink without cost from the spring
of the water of life."

REVELATION 21:6

FINDING BLESSINGS
IN THE RAIN

*T*hanksgiving or *complaining*—these words express two contrasting attitudes of the souls of God's children in regard to his dealings with them; and they are more powerful than we are inclined to believe in furthering or frustrating his purposes of comfort and peace toward us. The soul that complains can find comfort in nothing.

We cannot always give thanks for all things themselves, but we can always give thanks for God's love and care in the things that touch our lives. Not one thing can touch us except by his knowledge and permission. He is in them somewhere, and he is in them to compel, even the most grievous, to work together for our good and his glory. It is not because things are good that we are to thank the Lord, but because he is good. We are not wise enough to judge as to things, whether they are really, in their essence, joys or sorrows. But we always know that the Lord is good, and that his goodness makes it absolutely certain that everything he provides or permits must be good; and must therefore be something for which we would be heartily thankful, if only we could see it with his eyes.[9]

Hannah Whitall Smith

As above the darkest storm cloud
Shines the sun, serenely bright
Waiting to restore to nature
All the glory of his light,
So, behind each cloud of sorrow,
So, in each affliction, stands,
Hid, an angel, with a blessing
From the Father in his hand.
As without the tempest, pouring
O'er the earth the welcome rain,
All were but a fruitless desert,
Barren sand for ripen'ng grain,
So if ne'er a cloud of sadness
Veiled the sunshine of the soul,
If affliction's waves were never
Suffered o'er the heart to roll.
Love and faith might fail forever
To bring forth their fruits of peace;
Heaven's good seed of truth would perish
In a thorny wilderness.
So, with cloud and storm and tempest
Grows our earthly summer dim,
That the rebel heart, our Father
Thus may win to turn to Him.

Daniel H. Howard

Finding Blessings in the Rain

———

You, O LORD, keep my lamp burning;
  my God turns my darkness into light.

PSALM 18:28

We know that in all things God works for the good
of those who love him, who have been called
according to his purpose.

ROMANS 8:28

We also rejoice in our sufferings,
because we know that suffering produces
perseverance; perseverance,
character; and character, hope.

ROMANS 5:3–4

Dear friends, do not be surprised at the painful trial
you are suffering, as though something strange were
happening to you. But rejoice that you participate in the
sufferings of Christ, so that you may be overjoyed when
his glory is revealed. If you are insulted because of the
name of Christ, you are blessed, for the Spirit of glory
and of God rests on you.

1 PETER 4:12–14

WAITING FOR THE
STORM TO PASS

Many hours of waiting were necessary to enrich David's harp with song. And hours of waiting in the wilderness will provide us with psalms of "thanksgiving and the sound of singing." The hearts of the discouraged here below will be lifted, and joy will be brought to our Father's heavenly home.

What was the preparation for... David to compose songs unlike any others ever heard before on earth? It was the sinful persecution he endured at the hands of the wicked that brought forth his cries for God's help. Then David's faint hope in God's goodness blossomed into full songs of rejoicing, declaring the Lord's mighty deliverances and multiplied mercies....

One stinging sorrow spared would have been one blessing missed and unclaimed. One difficulty or danger escaped—how great would have been our loss! The thrilling psalms where God's people today find expression for their grief or praise might never have been known....

Therefore if God's desire is to enlarge your capacity for spiritual understanding, do not be frightened by the greater realm of suffering that awaits you. ... The breath of the Holy Spirit into his new creation never makes a heart hard and insensitive, but affectionate, tender, and true.[10]

Anna Shipton

Did you ever hear of anyone being much used for Christ who did not have some *special* waiting time, some complete *upset* of all his or her plans first; from St. Paul's being sent off into the desert of Arabia for three years, when he must have been boiling over with the glad tidings, down to the present day?

You were looking forward to telling about trusting Jesus in Syria; now he says, "I want to *show* what it is to trust me, without waiting for Syria."

My own case is far less severe, but the same in principle, that when I thought the door was flung open for me to go with a bound into literary work, it is opposed, and the doctor steps in and says, simply, "Never! She must choose between writing and living; she can't do both."

In 1869 [I] saw the evident wisdom of being kept waiting nine years in the shade. God's love being unchangeable, he is just as loving when we do not see or feel his love. Also his love and his sovereignty are co-equal and universal; so he withholds the enjoyment and conscious progress because he knows best what will really ripen and further his work in us.[11]

Frances Ridley Havergal

Waiting for the Storm to Pass

———

I wait for you, O LORD;
*   you will answer, O Lord my God.*

PSALM 38:15

I waited patiently for the LORD;
*   he turned to me and heard my cry.*
He lifted me out of the slimy pit,
*   out of the mud and mire;*
he set my feet on a rock
*   and gave me a firm place to stand.*

PSALM 40:1–2

The LORD longs to be gracious to you;
*   he rises to show you compassion.*
For the LORD is a God of justice.
*   Blessed are all who wait for him!*

ISAIAH 30:18

See how the farmer waits for the land to yield its valu-
able crop and how patient he is for the autumn and
spring rains. You too, be patient and stand firm, because
the Lord's coming is near.

JAMES 5:7–8

Shaken to the Foundations

The "foundation of God standeth sure" (2 Timothy 2:19 KJV), and it is the only foundation that does. Therefore, we need to be "shaken" from every other foundation in order that we may be forced to rest on the foundation of God alone. And this explains the necessity for those "shakings" through which so many Christians seem called to pass. The Lord sees that they are building their spiritual houses on flimsy foundations, which will not be able to withstand the "vehement beating" of the storms of life; and not in anger but in tenderest love, he shakes our earth and our heaven until all that "can be shaken" is removed, and only those "things which cannot be shaken" are left behind.

The apostle tells us that the things that are shaken are the "things that are made" (Hebrews 12:27 KJV); that is, the things that are manufactured by our own efforts, feelings that we get up, doctrines that we elaborate, good works that we perform. It is not that these things are bad things in themselves. It is only when the soul begins to rest on them instead of upon the Lord that he is compelled to "shake" us from off them. And this shaking applies, we are told, "not to the earth only, but also to heaven." This means, I am sure, that it is possible to have "things that are made" even in religious matters.

How much of the religiousness of many Christians consists of these "things that are made," I cannot say; but I sometimes think the great overturnings and tossings in matters of faith, which so distress Christians in these times, may be only the necessary shaking of the "things that are made," in order that only that which "cannot be shaken" may remain.[12]

Hannah Whitall Smith

Shaken to the Foundations

———

Now [God] has promised, "Once more I will shake not only the earth but also the heavens." The words "once more" indicate the removing of what can be shaken— that is, created things—so that what cannot be shaken may remain. Therefore, since we are receiving a king- dom that cannot be shaken, let us be thankful, and so worship God acceptably with reverence and awe.

HEBREWS 12:26–28

This is what the Sovereign LORD says:
"See, I lay a stone in Zion,
    a tested stone,
a precious cornerstone for a sure foundation;
    the one who trusts will never be dismayed."

ISAIAH 28:16

God's solid foundation stands firm.
2 Timothy 2:19

[Jesus said,] "Everyone who hears these words of mine and puts them into practice is like a wise man who built his house on the rock. The rain came down, the streams rose, and the winds blew and beat against that house; yet it did not fall, because it had its foundation on the rock."

MATTHEW 7:24–25

Be Still, My Soul

My soul, have you pondered these words: "Be still, and know" (Psalm 46:10)? In the hour of distress, you cannot hear the answer to your prayers. How often has the answer seemed to come much later! The heart heard no reply during the moment of its crying, its thunder, its earthquake, and its fire. But once the crying stopped, once the stillness came, once concern for other lives broke through the tragedy of your own life, the long-awaited reply appeared. You must rest, O soul, to receive your heart's desire. Slow the beating of your heart over concerns for your personal care. Place the storm of your individual troubles on God's altar of everyday trials, and the same night, the Lord will appear to you. His rainbow will extend across the subsiding flood, and in your stillness you will hear the everlasting music.[13]

From *Streams in the Desert*

God can accomplish anything. He can speak a word and grant desires. He said, "'Let there be light,' and there was light" (Genesis 1:3). God can give me peace with a glance. When a tumult of thoughts stir a storm within me, God can declare my soul to be still. All its tempests obey him.

When God works with me, I will fear no obstacle that earth or hell can put in my way.

Let nothing hide you from my sight. Let me look through everything and see you. Don't let me so much as glance in love or hope at anything below you. Let me understand that all of creation rests in the hollow of your hand. Let your hand be with me to keep me from evil. Let me live in your shadow. Then I will be secure. Then I will be sheltered.[14]

Elizabeth Singer Rowe

Being Still in My Soul

Why are you downcast, O my soul?
    Why so disturbed within me?
Put your hope in God,
    for I will yet praise him,
    my Savior and my God.

PSALM 42:5–6

I will be glad and rejoice in your love, [LORD,]
    for you saw my affliction
    and knew the anguish of my soul.

PSALM 31:7

The LORD your God is with you,
    he is mighty to save.
He will take great delight in you,
    he will quiet you with his love,
    he will rejoice over you with singing.

ZEPHANIAH 3:17

When anxiety was great within me,
    your consolation brought joy to my soul.

PSALM 94:19

Strengthened by the Storms

Some of life's storms—a great sorrow, a bitter disappointment, a crushing defeat—suddenly come upon us. Others may come slowly, appearing on the uneven edge of the horizon no larger than a person's hand. But trouble that seems so insignificant spreads until it covers the sky and overwhelms us.

Yet it is in the storm that God equips us for service. When God wants an oak tree, he plants it where the storms will shake it and the rains will beat down upon it. It is in the midnight battle with the elements that the oak develops its rugged fiber and becomes the king of the forest.

When God wants to make a person, he puts him into some storm. The history of humankind has always been rough and rugged. No one is complete until he has been out into the surge of the storm and has found the glorious fulfillment of the prayer, "O God, take me, break me, make me."

The beauties of nature come after the storm. The rugged beauty of the mountain is born in a storm, and the heroes of life are the storm-swept and battle-scarred.

You have been in the storms and swept by the raging winds. Have they left you broken, weary, and beaten in the valley, or have they lifted you to the sunlit summits of a richer, deeper, more abiding womanhood? Have they left you with more sympathy for the storm-swept and the battle-scarred?

The wind that blows can never kill
*   The tree God plants;*
It blows toward east, and then toward west,
The tender leaves have little rest,
But any wind that blows is best.
*   The tree that God plants*
Strikes deeper root, grows higher still,
Spreads greater limbs, for God's good will
*   Meets all its wants.*

There is no storm has power to blast
*   The tree God knows;*
No thunderbolt, nor beating rain,
Nor lightning flash, nor hurricane;
When they are spent, it does remain,
*   The tree God knows,*
Through every storm it still stands fast,
And from its first day to its last
*   Still fairer grows.*[15]

From *Streams in the Desert*

MEDITATIONS ON

Being Strengthened
by the Storms

———

*I will boast all the more gladly about my weaknesses,
so that Christ's power may rest on me. That is why,
for Christ's sake, I delight in weaknesses, in insults, in
hardships, in persecutions, in difficulties. For when
I am weak, then I am strong.*

2 CORINTHIANS 12:9–10

Do you not know?
    Have you not heard?
The LORD is the everlasting God,
    the Creator of the ends of the earth.
He will not grow tired or weary,
    and his understanding no one can fathom.
He gives strength to the weary
    and increases the power of the weak.
Even youths grow tired and weary,
    and young men stumble and fall;
but those who hope in the LORD
    will renew their strength.
they will soar on wings like eagles;
    they will run and not grow weary,
    they will walk and not be faint.

ISAIAH 40:28–31

In the Shepherd's Care

He maketh me to lie down in green pastures: he leadeth me beside the still waters.

Psalm 23:2 KJV

The shepherd is at the very center of the life of the sheep. He provides for their every need, satisfying them completely.

Sheep will not lie down if they have cause to be fearful. They are easily frightened. However, as soon as the shepherd appears and moves in the midst of the restless flock, they become quiet.

The lives of many Christians are filled with fear, bringing restlessness and frustration. Our Good Shepherd appears, saying, "Fear thou not; for I am with thee" (Isaiah 41:10 KJV). His presence in the midst of our need removes fear and gives rest.

Sheep will not lie down if they are hungry. The shepherd searches for the best pasture land available for his sheep. Our Good Shepherd knows we need to be well nourished for inner satisfaction. He provides nourishment for us from the green pastures of his Word. Nourished by it, we can lie down in quiet contentment.

Occasionally he has to MAKE us lie down. It may take illness, loneliness, heartache, or sorrow to accomplish this.

Not only does the shepherd lead his sheep in the green meadows of nourishment and rest, but beside the still waters. We are refreshed at the waters of quietness. The word for "still" waters can be translated "stilled" waters. Sheep will not drink from a rushing stream. They instinctively know that if their coat of wool becomes wet, they could drown. Sometimes the shepherd builds a little dam in a rushing stream to enable the flock to drink from "stilled" waters.

At times the swift moving streams of life almost engulf us. God has to dam up a quiet stream where we can come and drink deeply of the Water of Life. We may discover that the very circumstances dreaded most bring spiritual refreshment. Our Good Shepherd loves to see his sheep contented and relaxed, refreshed and satisfied with him.

Today are you nourished and refreshed? Are you fully satisfied? "Blessed are they which do hunger and thirst after righteousness: for they shall be filled" (Matthew 5:6 KJV).[16]

Millie Stamm

Being in the Shepherd's Care

———

[The LORD] tends his flock like a shepherd:
He gathers the lambs in his arms
and carries them close to his heart;
he gently leads those that have young.

ISAIAH 40:11

This is what the Sovereign LORD says: I myself will search
for my sheep and look after them. As a shepherd looks after
his scattered flock when he is with them, so will I look
after my sheep. I will rescue them from all the places
where they were scattered on a day of clouds and darkness.
... I will tend them in a good pasture, and the mountain
heights of Israel will be their grazing land. There they will
lie down in good grazing land, and there they will feed in a
rich pasture on the mountains of Israel. I myself will tend
my sheep and have them lie down, declares the Sovereign
LORD. I will search for the lost and bring back the strays.
I will bind up the injured and strengthen the weak.

EZEKIEL 34:11–12, 14–16

[Jesus said,] "I am the good shepherd; I know my sheep
and my sheep know me—just as the Father knows me and
I know the Father—and I lay down my life for the sheep."

JOHN 10:14-15

Even the Wind and the Waves Obey Him

I knew something was wrong as soon as I picked up the phone.

"I've just lost my job," my husband said.

"Oh, no! Why? What happened?" I tried to control the panic in my voice.

"Financial cutbacks," he said with a sigh. "I'm not the only one who's been let go."

Several days later I went to church for the dress rehearsal of the play I had written for the children's choir. One of my special little friends came running up to me and pressed something into my hand. "It's a gift for you. I got it at a garage sale."

"Oh, it's beautiful, Janeen," I said as I admired the blue sailboat pin. I fastened it to my blouse and gave her a hug.

The rest of the 25 choir members arrived and we began the rehearsal. They were all wound up, nervous, enthusiastic, and very loud as they sang our theme song: "I'm his kid and he's my best friend. He will never let me down...."

I believed those words when I wrote them. *Why*, I asked myself, *can't I believe them now?*

I glanced at the pin Janeen had given me. The sailboat reminded me of the storm on the Sea of Galilee, the terror that had gripped the disciples and the way Jesus calmed the sea.

I kept them afloat, just as I'm going to keep you afloat, I felt the Lord say.

Three months later my husband was still out of work. But we didn't go under. Some days the waves of worry and fear crashed in on me. I wondered if we'd ever again experience smooth sailing. Perhaps not. God never promised us a problem-free life. But he has promised always to be with us. We can know his peace in the midst of life's storms.[17]

Marlene Bagnull

MEDITATIONS ON

Even the Wind and the Waves Obey Him

---

*That day when evening came, [Jesus] said to his disciples,
"Let us go over to the other side."*

*Leaving the crowd behind, they took him along, just
as he was, in the boat. There were also other boats with
him. A furious squall came up, and the waves broke over
the boat, so that it was nearly swamped.*

*Jesus was in the stern, sleeping on a cushion. The dis-
ciples woke him and said to him, "Teacher, don't you care
if we drown?"*

*He got up, rebuked the wind and said to the waves,
"Quiet! Be still!" Then the wind died down and it was
completely calm.*

*He said to his disciples, "Why are you so afraid? Do
you still have no faith?"*

*They were terrified and asked each other, "Who is
this? Even the wind and the waves obey him!"*

MARK 4:35–41

They cried out to the LORD in their trouble,
*   and he brought them out of their distress.*
He stilled the storm to a whisper;
*   the waves of the sea were hushed.*
They were glad when it grew calm,
*   and he guided them to their desired haven.*
Let them give thanks to the LORD for his unfailing love
*   and his wonderful deeds for men.*

PSALM 107:28–31

AFTER THE STORM

As spring the winter doth succeed
And leaves the naked trees do dress,
The earth all black is clothed in green.
At sunshine each their joy express.

My sun's returned with healing wings,
My soul and body doth rejoice,
My heart exults and praises sings
To him that heard my wailing voice.

My winter's past, my storms are gone,
And former clouds seem now all fled,
But if they must eclipse again,
I'll run where I was succored.

I have a shelter from the storm,
A shadow from the fainting heat,
I have access unto his throne,
Who is a God so wondrous great.

O hath thou made my pilgrimage
Thus pleasant, fair, and good,
Blessed me in youth and elder age,
My Baca made a springing flood.

O studious am what I shall do
To show my duty with delight;
All I can give is but thine own
And at the most a simple mite.[18]

Anne Bradstreet

The winds and the waves obey Thy will,
Peace, be still!
Whether the wrath of the storm tossed sea,
Or demons or men, or whatever it be
No waters can swallow the ship where lies
The Master of ocean, and earth, and skies;
They all shall sweetly obey Thy will,
Peace, be still! Peace, be still!
They all shall sweetly obey Thy will,
Peace, peace, be still!

Master, the terror is over,
The elements sweetly rest;
Earth's sun in the calm lake is mirrored,
And heaven's within my breast;
Linger, O blessed Redeemer!
Leave me alone no more;
And with joy I shall make the blest harbor,
And rest on the blissful shore.

Mary A. Baker

After the Storm

———

The God of all grace, who called you to his eternal glory in Christ, after you have suffered a little while, will himself restore you and make you strong, firm and steadfast.

1 PETER 5:10

I consider that our present sufferings are not worth comparing with the glory that will be revealed in us.

ROMANS 8:18

Your attitude should be the same as that of Christ Jesus:
Who, being in very nature God,
    did not consider equality with God something
        to be grasped,
but made himself nothing,
    taking the very nature of a servant,
    being made in human likeness.
And being found in appearance as a man,
    he humbled himself
    and became obedient to death—
        even death on a cross!
Therefore God exalted him to the highest place
    and gave him the name that is above every name,
that at the name of Jesus every knee should bow,
    in heaven and on earth and under the earth,
and every tongue confess that Jesus Christ is Lord,
    to the glory of God the Father.

PHILIPPIANS 2:5–11

O God, make us children of quietness,
and heirs of peace.

Clement of Rome

*This is what the Sovereign LORD, the Holy One
of Israel, says:*
  *"In repentance and rest is your salvation,
    in quietness and trust is your strength."*

ISAIAH 30:15

O God, through the death of your Son, you
reconciled us one to another, drawing us together
in the bond of peace. In times of trouble and
adversity, may your peace sustain us, calming our
fretful and anxious hearts, and saving us from all
hateful and violent activities.

Ancient Prayer

*The LORD is good to those whose hope is in him,
    to the one who seeks him;
it is good to wait quietly
    for the salvation of the LORD.*

LAMENTATIONS 3:25–26

Keep your heart in peace; let nothing in this
world disturb it: everything has an end.

John of the Cross

Grace, mercy and peace from God the Father
and from Jesus Christ, the Father's Son, will be
with us in truth and love.

2 JOHN 1:3

I smiled to think God's greatness
Flowed around our incompleteness,
Round our restlessness His rest.

Elizabeth Barrett Browning

Peace reigns where our Lord reigns.

Julian of Norwich

The fruit of righteousness will be peace;
    the effect of righteousness will be
quietness and confidence forever.

ISAIAH 32:17

Like a river glorious is God's perfect peace,
Over all victorious in its bright increase;
Perfect, yet it floweth fuller every day,
Perfect, yet it groweth deeper all the way.
Stayed upon Jehovah, hearts are fully blest;
Finding, as he promised, perfect peace and rest.

Frances Ridley Havergal

Serenity

OF SPIRIT

FINDING A QUIET PLACE
IN A NOISY WORLD

Run to the
Strong Tower

And still the Queen kept crying, 'Faster! Faster!' but Alice felt she could not go faster, though she had no breath left to say so. The most curious part of the thing was, that the trees and the other things round them never changed their places at all. However fast they went, they never seemed to pass anything.

"Just as Alice was getting quite exhausted, they stopped. [She] looked around her in great surprise. 'Why, I do believe we've been under this tree the whole time! Everything's just as it was!'

"'Of course it is,' said the Queen. 'It takes all the running you can do, to keep in the same place. If you want to get somewhere else, you must run twice as fast as that!'"

Like Alice and the Red Queen in *Through the Looking-Glass*, we are a generation of women bent on running. Hurry there. Scurry there. Sprint to the office. Hustle the kids. Run by the neighbor's. Dash through the store. So much running, yet it seems we're getting nowhere. So much running, we feel like running away.

Where did we learn that relentless running is a virtue? Certainly we have responsibilities; certainly we must keep them. But how much is too much? How long can we run before we implode? Often "too much" arrives sooner than expected, and without time off we can burn out on short notice.

But I have good news. It's all right, even necessary, to run away from it all.

God invites us to run to him and then stop running, to hide out in his strong tower away from the clamoring world. The psalmist remembered,

> "In my distress I called to the LORD;
>   I cried to my God for help.
> From his temple he heard my voice;
>   my cry came before him, into his ears. ...
> He reached down from on high and took
>   hold of me;
>   he drew me out of deep waters"
> (Psalm 18:6, 16).

We may not be drowning in deep waters, but God knows that running aground—or even running in circles—feels just as perilous and exhausting. So he listens for our call; he wants to answer. He prepares a table for us each day, a feast of delight. He swings open the door; he desires that we enter in. He's willing to protect us from the foe even when the enemy is our self-made busyness. He promises to replenish our souls.[19]

Judith Couchman

Running to the Strong Tower

Send forth your light and your truth,
    let them guide me;
let them bring me to your holy mountain,
    to the place where you dwell.
Then will I go to the altar of God,
    to God, my joy and my delight.

PSALM 43:3–4

I call to God,
    and the LORD saves me.
Evening, morning and noon
    I cry out in distress,
        and he hears my voice.

PSALM 55:16–17

From the ends of the earth I call to you [LORD],
    I call as my heart grows faint;
    lead me to the rock that is higher than I.
For you have been my refuge,
    a strong tower against the foe.

PSALM 61:2–3

"I will refresh the weary and satisfy the faint,"
    says the LORD.

JEREMIAH 31:25

HEAVENLY REFRESHMENT

The dew is a source of freshness. It is nature's provision for renewing the face of the earth. It falls at night, and without it, vegetation would die. It is this great renewal value of the dew that is so often recognized in the Scriptures and used as a symbol of spiritual refreshment. Just as nature is bathed in dew, the Lord renews his people. In Titus 3:5 the same thought of spiritual refreshment is connected with the ministry of the Holy Spirit and referred to as "renewal by the Holy Spirit."

Many Christian workers do not recognize the importance of the heavenly dew in their lives, and as a result lack freshness and energy. Their spirits are withered and droopy for lack of dew.

Beloved fellow worker, you recognize the folly of a laborer attempting to work all day without eating, but do you recognize the folly of a servant of God attempting to minister without eating of the heavenly manna? Neither is it sufficient to have spiritual nourishment only occasionally.

Every day you must receive the "renewal by the Holy Spirit." You know the difference between your whole being pulsating with the energy and freshness of God's divine life or feeling worn-out and weary. Quietness and stillness bring the dew. At night when the leaves and grass are still, the plants' pores are open to receive the refreshing and invigorating bath. And spiritual dew comes from quietly lingering in the Master's presence. Get still before him, for haste will prevent you from receiving the dew. Wait before God until you feel saturated with his presence. Then move on to your next duty with the awareness of the freshness and energy of Christ.[20]

From *Streams in the Desert*

Heavenly Refreshment

May God give you of heaven's dew.

GENESIS 27:28

You gave abundant showers, O God;
*   you refreshed your weary inheritance.*

PSALM 68:9

When the kindness and love of God our Savior appeared,
he saved us, not because of righteous things we had done,
but because of his mercy. He saved us through the washing
of rebirth and renewal by the Holy Spirit, whom he poured
out on us generously through Jesus Christ our Savior.

TITUS 3:4–6

"As the rain and the snow
*   come down from heaven,*
and do not return to it
*   without watering the earth*
and making it bud and flourish,
*   so that it yields seed for the sower and bread for*
*   the eater,*
so is my word that goes out from my mouth:
*   It will not return to me empty,*
but will accomplish what I desire
*   and achieve the purpose for which I sent it,"*
*   [says the LORD.]*

ISAIAH 55:10–11

Like the Lilies
of the Field

To grow in grace is opposed to all growth in self-dependence or self-effort—to all legality, in fact, of every kind. It is to put our growing, as well as everything else, into the hands of the Lord and leave it with him. It is to be so satisfied with our [Caretaker], and with his skill and wisdom, that not a question will cross our minds as to his mode of treatment or his plan of cultivation. It is to grow as the lilies grow, or as the babies grow, without care and without anxiety; to grow by the power of an inward life-principle that cannot help but grow; to grow because we live, and therefore must grow; to grow because he who has planted us has planted a growing thing, and has made us on purpose to grow.

Surely this is what our Lord meant when he said, "Consider the lilies of the field, how they grow; they toil not, neither do they spin: And yet I say unto you, That even Solomon in all his glory was not arrayed like one of these" (Matthew 6:28–29 KJV).

Or when he says again, "Which of you by taking thought can add one cubit unto his stature?" (Matthew 6:27 KJV). There is no effort in the growing of a babe or of a lily. The lily does not toil nor spin, it does not stretch nor strain, it does not make any effort of any kind to grow, it is not conscious even that it is growing; but by an inward life-principle, and through the nurturing care of God's providence and the fostering of a caretaker or gardener, by the heat of the sun and the falling of the rain, it grows and buds and blossoms into the beautiful plant God meant it to be.[21]

Hannah Whitall Smith

Growing Like the Lilies of the Field

We pray ... that you may live a life worthy of the Lord and may please him in every way: bearing fruit in every good work, growing in the knowledge of God, being strengthened with all power according to his glorious might so that you may have great endurance and patience, and joyfully giving thanks to the Father, who has qualified you to share in the inheritance of the saints in the kingdom of light.

COLOSSIANS 1:10–12

Blessed is the man ...
[whose] delight is in the law of the LORD
     and on his law he mediatates day and night.
He is like a tree planted by streams of water,
     which yields its fruit in season
and whose leaf does not wither.
     Whatever he does prospers.

PSALM 1:1–3

The righteous will flourish like a palm tree,
     they will grow like a cedar of Lebanon;
planted in the house of the LORD,
     they will flourish in the courts of our God.

PSALM 92:12–13

YOUR WORDS
ARE LIKE HONEY

I stared at the paper fluttering across our driveway. It didn't resemble the usual throw outs. Hopping out of the car, I investigated. It looked like a tiny jelly roll.

As I opened the rolled-up paper, I sensed the gentle probing of God's Spirit: "This is only a message from man. Are you as eager these days to read God's message?"

Quickly, I defended myself: "I know that message. I've read the Bible all my life."

My spirit had been pricked, but curiosity won. The paper heralded the grand opening of a pizza parlor. I thought about it all afternoon. It whetted my appetite.

That evening my family and I visited the pizza parlor. The food looked yummy, but tasted like lead to me. I knew the Holy Spirit grieved over my flippant answer to his question, "Are you as eager to read God's message these days?"

Pushing down the pizza, I silently prayed, *Lord, that was a foolish reply. Knowing facts from the Bible isn't getting to know you. I've missed you this year. I need your love message. I want your counsel.*

Once again, joy bubbled inside me. But as we rode home I reflected on what had happened in the busyness of this year. Meaningful times with the Lord had dwindled. Off guard, my hunger and zest dried up. When I most needed spiritual nourishment, the enemy worked to keep me from it. He'd deceived me to think that only great chunks of time counted. Unable to read the Word of God that way, he kept me on guilt trips. Craftily, Satan led my mind astray from the simplicity of loving Jesus and valuing even a few of God's precious words.

As we drove into the driveway, my heart sang. The ever-faithful Holy Spirit had used a wisp of paper to whisper truth to my starving spirit. He took a tiny message, looking like a jelly roll, and pointed me back to the sweetness of my Savior.[22]

Neva B. True

Your Words Are Like Honey

The fear of the LORD is pure,
enduring forever.
The ordinances of the LORD are sure
and altogether righteous.
They are more precious than gold,
than much pure gold;
they are sweeter than honey,
than honey from the comb.

PSALM 19:9–10

How sweet are your words to my taste,
sweeter than honey to my mouth!

PSALM 119:103

When your words came, I ate them;
they were my joy and my heart's delight,
for I bear your name,
O LORD God Almighty.

JEREMIAH 15:16

Trust in the LORD with all your heart
and lean not on your own understanding;
in all your ways acknowledge him,
and he will make your paths straight....
This will bring health to your body
and nourishment to your bones.

PROVERBS 3:5–6, 8

The Comfort of a Mother's Love

God is happy to be our Father. God is pleased to be our Mother. God rejoices that he is our Spouse and our soul is his beloved. Christ is happy to be our Brother, and Jesus rejoices that he is our Savior. These make five great joys.

As truly as God is our Father, so also is God our Mother. God is both the power and goodness of fatherhood and the wisdom and lovingness of motherhood.

There are three ways to consider the motherhood of God. One is the foundation of the creation of our nature. The second is in the Incarnation, the taking of our human nature. The third is in motherhood at work.

The service rendered by a mother is naturally near, lovingly ready, and truly sure. We know that all our mothers experience pain for us. Jesus is our true Mother. He nourishes us. He alone loves and labors for us to the point of death.

When we realize our sin, we are embarrassed. We hide in shame. But our courteous Mother does not want us to run away. Nothing could be less pleasing to our Mother, who wants us to behave like a child. A hurt and distressed child runs to its mother for help.

Our lives are a wonderful mixture of happiness and grief. We possess both our risen Lord Jesus Christ and the disastrous results of Adam's fall.

We are all feeble children until our gracious Mother brings us up to our Father's joy. Then we will fully understand these words: All will be well. You will see for yourself that everything will be well.[23]

Julian of Norwich

the Comfort of a Mother's Love

———

"As a mother comforts her child,
*   so will I comfort you," [says the* LORD.]

ISAIAH 66:13

I have stilled and quieted my soul;
*   like a weaned child with its mother,*
*   like a weaned child is my soul within me.*
O Israel, put your hope in the LORD
*   both now and forevermore.*

PSALM 131:2–3

"Can a mother forget the baby at her breast
*   and have no compassion on the child she has borne?*
Though she may forget,
*   I will not forget you!*
See, I have engraved you on the palms of my
*   hands," [says the* LORD.]

ISAIAH 49:15–16

THE SERENITY OF
DAILY OFFERINGS

An exasperated friend once exclaimed, "I hate that life is so daily!"

I understand what she meant. In a perfect world, my life would be crammed with exotic places to visit, intriguing people to entertain, accolades for my creative work, plenty of leisure time, and enough money to finance it all.

That description isn't even close to reality.

While writing books, I'm cloistered in the house, away from friends and family, tapping on a computer keyboard and racking my brains for ideas. Readers of an author's newly released work may imagine publishing as glamorous, but for most writers it's a persistent plodding along. As my friend would say, a writer's life is "very daily." In other words, it's a continual grind with the possibility of always working in obscurity.

Life is this way for most of us. We experience highs and lows, but wedged in between are huge slices of ordinary, unacclaimed living. Sometimes we fear these times will stretch endlessly into the future, without purpose or meaning. We prefer variety and stimulation over the repetitive and mind-numbing nature of daily tasks.

Just how many times can we wash the dishes, add up numbers, drive the kids to school, or work at a machine without feeling insignificant?

With God, as many times as we need to.

These mundane days and tasks, like everything else in a believer's life, can be offered to God as sweet-smelling sacrifices. We can find meaning in them because we've given our lives, our very moments, our daily responsibilities to him. The kitchen, the office, the minivan, or the factory can serve as holy altars to God—places where we surrender, obey, and please him.

I love how this old poem expresses the delight of a soul accomplishing everyday tasks:

There are strange ways of serving God;
You sweep a room or turn a sod,
And suddenly, to your surprise,
You hear the whir of seraphim,
And find you're under God's own eyes
And building palaces for Him.

God has ordained our days, so we delight him by plodding through the ordinary times. And amazingly, we find him in the "dailyness" with us.[24]

Judith Couchman

the Serenity
of Daily Offerings

———

[Jesus said,] "If anyone would come after me, he must
deny himself and take up his cross daily and follow me.
For whoever wants to save his life will lose it,
but whoever loses his life for me will save it."

LUKE 9:23–24

To do what is right and just
    is more acceptable to the LORD than sacrifice.

PROVERBS 21:3

Through Jesus, therefore, let us continually offer to
God a sacrifice of praise—the fruit of lips that confess
his name. And do not forget to do good and to share
with others, for with such sacrifices God is pleased.

HEBREWS 13:15–16

I urge you,... in view of God's mercy, to offer your bodies
as living sacrifices, holy and pleasing to God—this is your
spiritual act of worship.

ROMANS 12:1

LIFT UP YOUR SOUL
IN THE MORNING

What a privilege to begin the day in the presence of God! It has been said, "The morning is one end of the thread on which the day's activities are strung and should be well-knotted with devotion." It makes a difference when we look into the face of God before going out to face people.

[In Psalm 5:2–3] we read something about David's prayer life. Out of a heart of love and worship he directed his prayer to God at the beginning of the day. He *lifted* his *voice* to God in prayer.

"Hearken unto the voice of my cry....

My voice shalt thou hear in the morning" (KJV). He began his day talking to God, confident that he would hear and answer.

Not only did the psalmist lift his voice, but he *lifted his heart* also. "In the morning will I direct my prayer unto thee." In the original Hebrew the expression "direct my prayer" implies coming to God with a prepared heart, a heart quieted from the hustle and bustle of the day, ready to listen to him.

Often we rush into and out of his presence without that quiet preparation of heart which is essential to communion with him.

"In the morning I prepare [a prayer, a sacrifice] for You and watch and wait [for You to speak to my heart]" (v. 3 AMP).

Lift your *heart* with your *voice* to God.

David's eyes followed the direction of his voice and heart: "and will *look up*." We may lift our voices to God but keep our eyes focused on our problems, our needs, our weaknesses and disappointments. When we lift our eyes, we see him. "And when they had lifted up their eyes, they saw no man, save Jesus only" (Matthew 17:8 KJV).[25]

Millie Stamm

MEDITATIONS ON

Lifting Up Your Soul
in the Morning

Let the morning bring me word of your unfailing love,
for I have put my trust in you.
Show me the way I should go, you [LORD]
for to you I lift up my soul.

PSALM 143:8

I will sing of your strength,
in the morning I will sing of your love;
for you are my fortress,
my refuge in times of trouble.
O my Strength, I sing praise to you;
you, O God, are my fortress, my loving God.

PSALM 59:16–17

Satisfy us in the morning with your unfailing love,
that we may sing for joy and be glad all our days.

PSALM 90:14

O LORD, be gracious to us;
we long for you.
Be our strength every morning,
our salvation in time of distress.

ISAIAH 33:2

THE SOUL'S TRUE TREASURE

Gather, O Lord, my senses and the powers of my soul together in yourself. Pardon me and forgive me as often as I pray without concentrating on you. Many times I am not really at the place where I am standing or sitting. My thoughts carry me to some other place. I am where my thought is. I love what I think about.

If I love heaven, I speak gladly of the things of God.

If I love the world, I love to talk of worldly things.

If I love the flesh, I imagine things that please the flesh.

If I love my soul, I delight in talk about things that are for my soul's health.

Whatever I love, I gladly hear and speak of it. I fantasize about it. Jesus was right when he said, "For where your treasure is, there your heart will be also" (Matthew 6:21).[26]

From *Near to the Heart of God*

Lord Jesus, help me to want what is most pleasant to you. You know what is best for me. Give what you will, when the right time comes, and in the quantity you prefer. Do with me as you please. Put me where you will. I am in your hands. I am your servant. I am ready to do whatever you command. You are the true peace of my heart and the perfect rest of my soul.

If you want me to be in light, I will praise you. If you want me to be in darkness, I will also praise you.

If you comfort me, I will bless you. If you allow me to be troubled, I will bless you.

O Lord, make possible by your grace that which is impossible by my nature.

Sometimes I think I am going to hold together, but when a little trouble comes it tears me apart. Good Lord, you know my weakness, my frailness. Have mercy on me.[27]

Catherine Parr

the Soul's True Treasure

———

[Jesus said,] "Do not store up for yourselves treasures on earth, where moth and rust destroy, and where thieves break in and steal. But store up for yourselves treasures in heaven, where moth and rust do not destroy, and where thieves do not break in and steal. For where your treasure is, there your heart will be also."

MATTHEW 6:19–21

Those who know your name will trust in you,
     for you, LORD, have never forsaken those who seek you.

PSALM 9:10

One thing I ask of the LORD,
     this is what I seek:
that I may dwell in the house of the LORD
     all the days of my life,
to gaze upon the beauty of the LORD
     and to seek him in his temple.

PSALM 27:4

[The Lord] will be the sure foundation for your times,
     a rich store of salvation and wisdom and knowledge;
     the fear of the LORD is the key to this treasure.

ISAIAH 33:6

LISTEN FOR HIS
QUIET SONG

In his novel *Whalesong*, Robert Siegel weaves an endearing and imaginative tale about a family of humpback whales. A few pages into the novel the reader learns that whales are good listeners. They listen intently for communication, in the form of a song, from other members of the pod. ...

Siegel's whales listen to locate one another, to navigate while traveling in groups, and to ensure protection against attackers. They listen as an expression of love and as a means to preserve families and communities. For me they illustrate that throughout the animal kingdom, listening plays a crucial role to survival.

I've seen these marine mammals spout water and jump playfully off the East Coast, but I really only need the backyard to watch creatures listening. Birds flutter and fly when my cat slinks nearby; the cat perks her ears and hides when a dog approaches; the dog listens for car sounds before crossing a street. Observing nature's instincts, I wonder, *Why is it so hard for people to listen, to do what even the animals know is important for survival?*

We might try to hear one another, we may even occasionally listen to our own souls, but we often neglect listening to God. Yet he is the one we depend on for physical and spiritual survival, the one who woos and nurtures, warns and corrects, guides and sustains us. So why don't we listen? Why don't we hear?

Perhaps we don't understand that he is the voice of compassion and protection. We don't realize he is the comforter, the giver of good gifts, the ever-attentive lover of our souls. He is not the distant father, the critical mother, the man who emotionally or physically left us. He is God and God is love.

Yes, it must be a misunderstanding. We must be confusing him with somebody else. Why else would we be too busy or afraid to listen? (Why else would the animals be smarter than us?) Why else would we refuse the sound of love?[28]

Judith Couchman

Listening for His Quiet Song

He put a new song in my mouth,
     a hymn of praise to our God.
Many will see and fear
     and put their trust in the LORD.

PSALM 40:3

[Jesus said,] "My sheep listen to my voice; I know them,
and they follow me."

JOHN 10:27

By day the LORD directs his love,
     at night his song is with me—
     a prayer to the God of my life.

PSALM 42:8

You turned my wailing into dancing;
     you removed my sackcloth and clothed me with joy,
that my heart may sing to you and not be silent.
     O LORD my God, I will give you thanks forever.

PSALM 30:11–12

I will listen to what God the LORD will say;
     he promises peace to his people, his saints.

PSALM 85:8

QUIET TIME WITH
YOUR FATHER

Christ Jesus, in his humanity, felt the need of complete solitude—to be entirely by himself, alone with himself. Each of us knows how draining constant interchange with others can be and how it exhausts our energy. As part of humankind, Jesus knew this and felt the need to be by himself in order to regain his strength. Solitude was also important to him in order to fully realize his high calling, his human weakness, and his total dependence on his Father.

As a child of God, how much more do we need times of complete solitude—times to deal with the spiritual realities of life and to be alone with God the Father. If there was ever anyone who could dispense with special times of solitude and fellowship, it was our Lord. Yet even he could not maintain his full strength and power for his work and his fellowship with the Father without his quiet time.

God desires that every servant of his would understand and perform this blessed practice, that his church would know how to train its children to recognize this high and holy privilege, and that every believer would realize the importance of making time for God alone.

Oh, the thought of having God all alone to myself and knowing that God has me all alone to himself!

Have you ever pictured yourself as the last remaining person on earth, or the only person left in the entire universe? If you were the only person remaining in the universe, your every thought would be, "God and I! God and I!" And yet he is already as close to you as that. He is as near as if no heart but his and yours ever beat throughout the boundlessness of space.[29]

From *Streams in the Desert*

Quiet Time with Your Father

___

As the deer pants for streams of water,
*   so my soul pants for you, O God.*
My soul thirsts for God, for the living God.
*   When can I go and meet with God?*

PSALM 42:1–2

Jesus made the disciples get into the boat and go on
ahead of him to the other side, while he dismissed the
crowd. After he had dismissed them, he went up on a
mountainside by himself to pray. When evening came,
he was there alone.

MATTHEW 14:22–23

The news about Jesus spread all the more, so that crowds
of people came to hear him and to be healed of their sick-
nesses. But Jesus often withdrew to lonely places and prayed.

LUKE 5:15–16

[Jesus said,] "When you pray, go into your room, close the
door and pray to your Father, who is unseen. Then your
Father, who sees what is done in secret, will reward you."

MATTHEW 6:6

His Still, Small Voice

One way God can awaken a soul is with an inner voice. This "voice" comes in many ways and is difficult to define.

The inner voice I speak of can come from God, from the devil, or from one's own imagination. Do not think you are a better person because you sense this inner voice—even if it is genuinely from God. The only good that results is in how you respond to what you hear. If what you hear is not in agreement with the Scriptures, pay no attention to it at all.

There are some clues that will help you to determine if God is the source. The first and best indication is in the *power and authority* of the voice. Things are better because it was heard. Some difference is made—calmness replaces distress, for instance.

The second sign is a *peaceful tranquility* in the soul combined with an eagerness to sing praises to God.

The third sign is that the words *stick in the memory* better than ordinary conversation. There is a strong faith in the truth of what was heard. Even if all the evidence indicates that the soul misunderstood, and much time passes, there is still confidence that God will find his own way to fulfill his promises.

Delays may cause doubts. The devil will actually prey upon your doubts. He will work hard to intimidate you if the inner voice spoke of something challenging that will bring honor to God. In spite of all these difficulties, there will remain a glowing ember of faith that God will overcome all obstacles and keep his word.

Now if the inner voice is only the product of the imagination, none of these signs will be present. There will be no certainty, no peace, no joy.

If what you think is an "inner voice" commands an action that will have dire consequences for yourself or for others, don't do anything until you have sought competent counseling.

Teresa of Avila

Lord, let your Holy Spirit inspire me. Make me receptive. But please, Lord God, spare me from assigning your name to the complex thoughts, desires, and motives of my own personality. Amen.[30]

His Still, Small Voice

———

Whether you turn to the right or to the left,
your ears will hear a voice behind you, saying,
"This is the way; walk in it."

ISAIAH 30:21

[Jesus said,] "Here I am! I stand at the door and knock.
If anyone hears my voice and opens the door, I will
come in and eat with him, and he with me."

REVELATION 3:20

This is how you can recognize the Spirit of God:
Every spirit that acknowledges that Jesus Christ
has come in the flesh is from God.

1 JOHN 4:2

Show me your ways, O LORD,
teach me your paths;
guide me in your truth and teach me,
for you are God my Savior,
and my hope is in you all day long.

PSALM 25:4–5

LONGING TO BE SATISFIED

While David was alone in the wilderness he was evidently reminiscing of the time when God had been very real to him in the sanctuary. He still desired the reality of God's presence that he had known in the past. He said, "O God, thou art MY God." From the depths of his soul he cried out,

"My soul thirsteth for THEE, my flesh longeth for THEE in a dry and thirsty land, where no water is" (Psalm 63:1 KJV).

The story is told of a Thai man who came to a Thailand mission station. They said to him, "Are you looking for some medicine?"

"No," he replied, "I am looking for God."

There are many hungers and thirsts in the world today. Some people hunger for position; some for power. Others hunger for pleasure, love, or acceptance. People are searching everywhere for things that will satisfy. But inner satisfaction does not come through things. Jesus assures us that the hunger and thirst of our soul can be satisfied. "Blessed are they which do hunger and thirst after righteousness: for they shall be filled" (Matthew 5:6 KJV).

Inner fulfillment comes from HIM. David said, "Early will I seek HIM." When we read the Bible we must seek him on its pages. When we enter the prayer closet we must become quiet enough to hear him speak to us. We must not stop short of anything less than God himself.

Today, are you seeking inner peace? Are you longing for something to satisfy? You can be satisfied; you can have inner fulfillment as you seek and find it in Jesus Christ. He said, "If any man thirst, let him come unto me, and drink" (John 7:37 KJV).

Tell HIM today of the longing of your heart. Seek him from the Word of God. Talk to him, and let him talk to you in prayer.

Your inner longing can be satisfied in him today.[31]

Millie Stamm

Longing to Be Satisfied

My soul faints with longing for your salvation,
*   but I have put my hope in your word.*

PSALM 119:81

Jesus declared, "I am the bread of life. He who comes
to me will never go hungry, and he who believes in
me will never be thirsty."

JOHN 6:35

In righteousness I will see your face;
*   when I awake, I will be satisfied with seeing*
*   your likeness.*

PSALM 17:15

Let them give thanks to the LORD for his unfailing love
*   and his wonderful deeds for men,*
for he satisfies the thirsty
*   and fills the hungry with good things.*

PSALM 107:8–9

Precious Letters

Eagerly I went to the mailbox—again. Why was the mail so late today? Impatiently I searched up and down the street to see if I could see the mailman coming. He was nowhere to be seen.

I went back to the kitchen, but couldn't settle down to get anything done. Then I thought I heard the lid of my mailbox squeak. I rushed down the stairs and opened the door. Sure enough! There was a letter from my husband!

I read that letter about five times that afternoon. It was so good to imagine him talking to me. He was in the primitive country of Irian Jaya—on the other side of the world. To make a phone call was terribly expensive and just about impossible to do. So we had to be content with letters.

This letter made so much difference in my day. I was at peace and felt loved. It was so good to know that he was fine and the work was progressing nicely. His work was nearing completion and he would be back home again soon.

As I put the letter down, my eyes fell on my Bible. I had bought it a year ago and it still looked new. It seemed as if I could hear God saying, "My child, I have written some letters to you as well, but you have not read them so eagerly. I want to talk to you, too. I want to assure you that I love you. I want to make a difference in your day.

"It won't be long now until I come back. And when I do, I want to find you unashamed and ready to return with me, so that where I am, there you may be also. I want you to rest in me and not let your heart become troubled. Enjoy my peace, child."

Dear Father, please help me to be faithful in reading your letters and obeying your directions. Thank you for your love and your peace. I want to trust you more. Amen.[32]

Beryl Henne

Precious Letters

As for God, his way is perfect;
the word of the LORD is flawless.

PSALM 18:30

The precepts of the LORD are right,
giving joy to the heart.
The commands of the LORD are radiant,
giving light to the eyes.

PSALM 19:8

I delight in your commands,
because I love them.

PSALM 119:47

[Jesus said,] "If you remain in me and my words remain in
you, ask whatever you wish, and it will be given you. This
is to my Father's glory, that you bear much fruit, showing
yourselves to be my disciples. As the Father has loved me,
so have I loved you. Now remain in my love. If you obey
my commands, you will remain in my love, just as I have
obeyed my Father's commands and remain in his love."

JOHN 15:7–10

Let the word of Christ dwell in you richly.

COLOSSIANS 3:16

QUIET CONVERSATIONS

The Bible encourages us to pray continually, but how can we accomplish this? We've so many activities to do and think about, how do we keep up with God, too?

God dwells with us continually, so we can consider him a companion, with us wherever we go. Conversations with a companion usually divide into two categories: maintaining and probing. In maintenance conversations we ask questions to receive quick information, comment on everyday occurrences, listen while our hands keep busy, tell funny and interesting stories, give necessary (and sometimes unnecessary) instructions, mention topics that need more discussion later, or say, "How's it going?" when we can only see each other periodically. We converse through the flow of a day, responding to events and maintaining the relationship.

Probing conversations *are* events. We stop and talk more deeply and meaningfully. We hear, listen, and respond more carefully. We wrestle with problems, explain our requests, review our days, catch up on current thinking, explore each other's desires, seek definitive answers and activities, affirm our hopes and plans. These conversations affect our well-being, self-esteem, and sense of direction. They grow a relationship and feed the soul.

Through prayer we can conduct both kinds of conversations with God. In either case, an effective conversationalist commits herself to talking and listening, hearing and responding, being honest and trustworthy, keeping the channels open and free from obstructions. ...

When we assume our responsibility in this two-way commitment, our prayer changes from something rote into real communication, into a living relationship with God.

Listening God, I want to dialogue with you all day long today. I want to speak and wait to hear your response. I want our conversations to be like no other communication in my life. Day by day, step by step, help me to build a prayerful relationship with you. [33]

Judith Couchman

Quiet Conversations

"Before [my people] call I will answer;
*   while they are still speaking I will hear," [says the LORD.]*

ISAIAH 65:24

I call on you, O God, for you will answer me;
*   give ear to me and hear my prayer.*

PSALM 17:6

How gracious [God] will be when you cry for help! As
soon as he hears, he will answer you.

ISAIAH 30:19

God has surely listened
*   and heard my voice in prayer.*
Praise be to God,
*   who has not rejected my prayer*
*   or withheld his love from me!*

PSALM 66:19–20

Do not be anxious about anything, but in everything, by
prayer and petition, with thanksgiving, present your
requests to God. And the peace of God, which transcends
all understanding, will guard your hearts and your minds
in Christ Jesus.

PHILIPPIANS 4:6–7

PEACE FOR A
RESTLESS HEART

Dear restless heart, be still; don't fret and worry so;
God has a thousand ways His love to help and show;
Just trust, and trust, and trust, until His will you know.

Dear restless heart, be still, for peace is God's own smile.
His love can every wrong and sorrow reconcile;
Just love, and love, and love, and calmly wait awhile.

Dear restless heart, be brave; don't moan and sorrow so,
He has a meaning kind in chilly winds that blow;
Just hope, and hope, and hope, until you braver grow.

Dear restless heart, recline upon His breast this hour,
His grace is strength and life, His love is bloom and
flower;
Just rest, and rest, and rest, within His tender power.

Dear restless heart, be still! Don't struggle to be free;
God's life is in your life, from Him you may not flee;
Just pray, and pray, and pray, till you have faith to see.[34]

Edith Willis Linn

The Quiet Hour

Speak, Lord, in the stillness
While I wait on Thee;
Hushed my heart to listen,
In expectancy.

Speak, O blessed Master,
In this quiet hour,
Let me see Thy face, Lord,
Feel Thy touch of power.

For the words Thou speakest,
"They are life" indeed;
Living Bread from heaven,
Now my spirit feed!

All to Thee is yielded,
I am not my own;
Blissful, glad surrender,
I am Thine alone.

Fill me with the knowledge
Of Thy glorious will;
All Thine own good pleasure
In my life fulfill.

Like "a watered garden"
Full of fragrance rare
Ling'ring in Thy presence
Let my life appear.

E. May Grimes

Peace for a Restless Heart

———

*[Jesus said,] "Do not let your hearts be troubled.
Trust in God; trust also in me."*

JOHN 14:1

A heart at peace gives life to the body.

PROVERBS 14:30

*I will lie down and sleep in peace,
    for you alone, O LORD,
        make me dwell in safety.*

PSALM 4:8

*God is just: He will pay back trouble to those who
trouble you and give relief to you who are troubled.*

2 THESSALONIANS 1:6–7

*[Jesus said,] "Peace I leave with you; my peace I give
you. I do not give to you as the world gives. Do not let
your hearts be troubled and do not be afraid."*

JOHN 14:27

QUIET REST
IN A NOISY WORLD

Times change, but our basic needs remain stable. We need rest. You should see my neighbor. While I rush through one job with my mind on the next in line, she just drops down on the grass, idly chewing a pepperwood stem. "I'm unable to finish all that needs doing today, so what's the rush?"

"I accomplish more if I sit a spell—not working just thinking and appreciating." Let life settle around you.

Somewhere there's a recipe for people like me who try to do a year's work in one day—and rob themselves of "thinking time." My friend reads, "so I can know the hopes and dreams in a world before my time," she says. My friend listens to music "so I can enlarge my heart and mind." My friend prays "so I can enlarge the soul." Her philosophy is contagious.

We can't change our patterns with one sitting, but one is a beginning! Today I tried it just once. When the pressure became unbearable, I just stopped, looked, listened and sniffed—like the watchful and appreciative family boxer who dropped in the grass alongside me, his bobbed-off tail fanning in a flurry of sheer joy. "Lord, it is good to be here," I whispered, remembering that God and his mysterious seasons remain the same.

Take fifteen minutes; look at the lovely things you miss by rushing. Return to the mechanics of living refreshed, God's way.

We miss so much when we rush through
A meditation-walk:
The seas of grass in golden wheat,
The silver willow's talk,
A child at play in scented hay,
A birdsong in the trees
Are whispers straight from God, I think.
"Why hurry and miss these?"
From rosy dawn till day is gone
Beyond some lofty crest,
Sight, scent, and sound are gifts of God
We miss unless we rest.[35]

June Masters Bacher

Quiet Rest in a Noisy World

My soul finds rest in God alone;
my salvation comes from him.

PSALM 62:1

The apostles gathered around Jesus and reported to him
all they had done and taught. Then, because so many
people were coming and going that they did not even
have a chance to eat, he said to them, "Come with me
by yourselves to a quiet place and get some rest." So they
went away by themselves in a boat to a solitary place.

MARK 6:30–32

The fear of the LORD leads to life:
Then one rests content, untouched by trouble.

PROVERBS 19:23

[Jesus said,] "Come to me, all you who are weary and
burdened, and I will give you rest. Take my yoke upon
you and learn from me, for I am gentle and humble in
heart, and you will find rest for your souls."

MATTHEW 11:28–29

Come ye yourselves apart and rest awhile;
Weary, I know it, of the press and throng,
Wipe from your brow the sweat and dust of toil,
And in My quiet strength again be strong.

Edward H. Bickersteth, Jr.

To the heart that knows Thy love, O Purest!
There is a temple, sacred evermore,
And all the babble of life's angry voices
Dies in hushed stillness at its peaceful door.

Far, far away, the roar of passion dies,
And loving thoughts rise calm and peacefully,
And no rude storm, how fierce so e'er it flies,
Disturbs the soul that dwells, O Lord, in Thee.

O Rest of rests! O Peace, serene, eternal!
Thou ever livest, and Thou changest never;
And in the secret of Thy presence dwells
Fullness of joy, for ever and for ever.

Harriet Beecher Stowe

It is good to live in the valley sweet,
Where the work of the world is done,
Where the reapers sing in the fields of wheat,
And work till the setting of the sun.
But beyond the meadows, the hills I see
Where the noises of traffic cease,
And I follow a Voice who calls out to me
From the hilltop regions of peace.

Yes, to live is sweet in the valley fair,
And work till the setting of the sun;
But my spirit yearns for the hilltop's air
When the day and its work are done.
For a Presence breathes o'er the silent hills,
And its sweetness is living yet;
The same deep calm all the hillside fills,
As breathed over Olivet.[36]

From *Streams in the Desert*

I lift up my eyes to the hills—
    where does my help come from?
My help comes from the LORD,
    the Maker of heaven and earth.

PSALM 121:1–2

Passing
THE PEACE

GIVING TO OTHERS FROM THE
TRANQUILITY IN YOUR HEART

Reaping a Harvest
of Love

My VW couldn't hold another person. I had taken several widows to church and returned to pick up some children. A family of six made a carload. One Sunday morning, a little girl stood by and watched as the children climbed aboard. She looked so lonely standing there.

Even though the car was full, I asked if she wanted to go to church with us. She said she would ask her mother if she could go next week. She did go next week, and every Sunday for some time.

That was many years ago. I'm now in my golden years; old age has taken its toll. Life is lonely; two of my children have preceded me in death. I am fearful of the future without daughters to care for me. Old age can be a time of fear and frustration, even with the Lord's presence. To occupy my time, I have become a member of the prayer chain at church. I can do this from my rocking chair.

One day, I received a call to pray for a woman in need. In turn, I phoned her to ask if she'd like to come to my house for prayer.

When I answered the door, she threw her arms around me and began to cry. Through her tears, she told me she was the little girl I had taken to church years before. We prayed, and God met her need.

She comes to see me often now. She drives me to church, runs errands for me and cooks little "goodies" to cheer me up. She has become such a blessing!

Harvest time comes to all of us. We really do reap what we sow. If we plant the seeds of hate, greed, envy and strife, we can expect a harvest of the same. Years ago, I planted a seed in the heart of a small girl, and now I am reaping a harvest of love.[37]

Josephine Smith

Reaping a Harvest of Love

He who sows righteousness reaps a sure reward.

PROVERBS 11:18

Sow for yourselves righteousness,
*   reap the fruit of unfailing love,*
and break up your unplowed ground;
*   for it is time to seek the* LORD,
until he comes
*   and showers righteousness on you.*

HOSEA 10:12

Peacemakers who sow in peace raise a harvest
of righteousness.

JAMES 3:18

Let us not become weary in doing good, for at the
proper time we will reap a harvest if we do not give up.

GALATIANS 6:9

Remember this: Whoever sows sparingly will
also reap sparingly, and whoever sows generously
will also reap generously.

2 CORINTHIANS 9:6

JUST A LITTLE
BIT OF TIME

The pink-blanketed bundle was still in the quickly improvised apple-box crib. I tip-toed over and touched the pudgy pink face with my index finger—the way I used to when I would awaken from a needed night's sleep and wonder if my own son had swallowed his tongue or suffocated in his zipped-up cover. It was a world revisited for me. It has been a long time since I have handled a baby. I had volunteered to help the young mother whose sister was ill.

The forehead was reassuringly warm. Too warm? I pushed aside the covers. Was Bryce ever that small; his fingers (which flailed at my touch) that wee? The baby's blue eyes, tightly squeezed together, trembled. The lips pursed and smacked—quivering into a smile just as his eyes flickered open. I smiled back, exhaling in relief—the way I did a quarter of a century ago. As I was leaving to get back to my work, there was a wail. A safety pin? It couldn't be, they wear Pampers now. The wail stopped when the baby's eyes tried to focus on my face. Wet? No.

"What's the problem, fellow?" The answer was a coo. And I turned to go out again. "Please," I prayed.

This time there was a howl. Something was wrong! Should I call the pediatrician? Where was the schedule? Was it time for the baby's formula or orange juice? I grabbed both and ran back into the room. The howl reduced to a gurgle as I stood over the crib. The sly little fellow saw me for an easy mark. Fat arms and two sleeper-clad feet went into an arc—he wanted to be held. I knew it would do no good to show him the mobile of butterflies or offer him food, but I tried.

Something triggered a memory of Bryce on his fourth birthday. He'd eaten too much birthday cake; he was tired of his gifts, and he was screaming! "All I want is a little bitta time!" I took him into my arms where he promptly fell asleep. But at six weeks old? I reached for this one with remembered skill. The tiny head drooped and the smile was back.

How many new lives, fresh and shining; how many old lives, worn and drab, are in need of a little bit of our time?[38]

June Masters Bacher

Just a Little Bit of Time

———

*[Jesus said,] "If anyone gives even a cup of cold water
to one of these little ones because he is my disciple,
I tell you the truth, he will certainly not lose his reward."*

MATTHEW 10:42

*Be completely humble and gentle; be patient, bearing
with one another in love.*

EPHESIANS 4:2

*Share with God's people who are in need.
Practice hospitality.*

ROMANS 12:13

*[Jesus said,] "Love one another. As I have loved you,
so you must love one another."*

JOHN 13:34

The Right Words at the Right Time

Five o'clock at last; I [stacked a few papers and pushed in my desk chair.] As I did, Sharon, the secretary who sat at the desk next to mine, lingered around my work area. It was obvious by the way she picked up a pen and put it down again that something was on her mind.

With a smile, I sighed, "Long day, wasn't it?"

"How does God speak to you?" Sharon blurted out.

"Through Scripture and prayers," I answered after a brief hesitation. "He ... He ... sometimes ..." My mind went blank.

Before I had a chance to say another word, Sharon grabbed her purse and was out the door, barely taking time to toss a "Good night ... thanks," over her shoulder.

It never failed. Every time Sharon asked me about God or salvation, I was only able to answer her specific question, and then couldn't think of another thing to say.

I'd been trying to lead Sharon to the Lord for several months and even though I'd brought her to church and introduced her to my friends, I felt I was failing her—and God. And even though I believed God can turn everything to good, I wondered how he could use my silence to his advantage.

One morning several days later, Sharon came running over to me. Her sparkling eyes told me something wonderful had happened.

"I accepted the Lord last night," she said, as she reached over and grabbed my hand. She explained how one her new friends at church had prayed with her. Smiling, she continued, "Thanks for not preaching to me when I asked questions. Everyone else tried to tell me too much at one time, and I became confused. You simply answered my questions, and told me what I needed to know at the time."

I smiled to myself when Sharon went back to her own desk. God's ways are so mysterious and powerful. He can even use silence to his advantage.[39]

Beverly Hamilton

the Right Words at the Right Time

———

May the words of my mouth and the meditation
of my heart
    be pleasing in your sight,
      O LORD, my Rock and my Redeemer.

PSALM 19:14

The lips of the righteous nourish many.

PROVERBS 10:21

Pleasant words are a honeycomb,
    sweet to the soul and healing to the bones.

PROVERBS 16:24

Reckless words pierce like a sword,
    but the tongue of the wise brings healing.

PROVERBS 12:18

If anyone speaks, he should do it as one speaking
the very words of God.

1 PETER 4:11

THE VALUE OF
WASTING TIME

My friend Susan calls and says she's on her way to Starbucks for coffee. Will I join her?

"No, no," I say. "I'm still in my robe. It'd take too much time to get ready and get together. This morning I need to write."

As I hang up the phone, I think, *It would have been nice to go. My work-at-home schedule is flexible. Why is it so hard for me to say yes?* For some reason, I think it's more virtuous to stick with my work than to spend an hour with a friend. An inner voice says I'd be wasting time, but do these words speak the truth?

I don't believe that time spent cultivating a relationship, those moments or hours passed with meaningful people, is wasted. Especially not time with someone as interesting and vital to me as Susan. Especially not when I spend day after day alone to write.

So what really stops me from hovering together over coffee? ...

When I "waste" valuable time with Susan— if I hang out at her favorite coffee shop and listen to her life—I express my love. I show she's more valuable than a manuscript. I touch her soul and she reaches into mine.

"Throwing away" time with Susan expresses love to myself too. Being together refreshes my brain, reignites my creativity, and reaffirms who I am in the world. I return to my work recharged.

So I ask myself again, What stops me from buying that cup of coffee?

The answer is neither poetic nor sensible, as I would hope.

The answer is that I've developed a bad habit.

I'm in the habit of saying no, thinking it more efficient to work and "not waste my time." But for the sake of my soul and its relationships, I need to develop the habit of "wasting time" on people, of throwing away a precious commodity to love them as Christ does, of refilling my cup when I'm empty.

[Jesus tells us to] "Give, and it will be given to you. A good measure pressed down, shaken together and running over, will be poured into your lap. For with the measure you use, it will be measured to you" (Luke 6:38).

Starbucks is still open. I'm going to call Susan.[40]

Judith Couchman

the Value of Wasting Time

———

Let us not give up meeting together, as some are in the habit of doing, but let us encourage one another.

HEBREWS 10:25

A generous man will prosper;
*   he who refreshes others will himself be refreshed.*

PROVERBS 11:25

As we have opportunity, let us do good to all people, especially to those who belong to the family of believers.

GALATIANS 6:10

Let no debt remain outstanding, except the continuing debt to love one another.

ROMANS 13:8

BEAUTIFUL FEET

Our Lord has many uses for what is kept for himself. How beautiful are the feet of them that bring glad tidings of good things! That is the best use of all, and I expect the angels think those feet beautiful, even if they are cased in muddy boots or galoshes.

If we want to have these beautiful feet, we must have the tidings ready which they are to bear. Let us ask him to keep our hearts so freshly full of his good news of salvation that our mouths may speak out of their abundance. If the clouds be full of rain, they empty themselves upon the earth. May we be so filled with the Spirit that we may have much to pour out for others.

Besides the privilege of carrying water from the wells of salvation, there are plenty of cups of cold water to be carried in all directions; not to the poor only—ministries of love are often as much needed by a rich friend. But the feet must be kept for these; they will be too tired for them if they are tired out for self-pleasing. In such services we are treading in the blessed steps of Christ, who went about doing good.[41]

Frances Ridley Havergal

Take My Life and Let It Be

Take my life, and let it be consecrated, Lord, to Thee.
Take my moments and my days; let them flow in
ceaseless praise.
Take my hands, and let them move at the impulse
of Thy love.
Take my feet, and let them be swift and beautiful
for Thee.

Take my voice, and let me sing always, only,
for my King.
Take my lips, and let them be filled with messages
from Thee.
Take my silver and my gold; not a mite would I
withhold.
Take my intellect, and use every power as Thou
shalt choose.

Take my will, and make it Thine; it shall be no
longer mine.
Take my heart, it is Thine own; it shall be Thy
royal throne.
Take my love, my Lord, I pour at Thy feet its
treasure store.
Take myself, and I will be ever, only, all for Thee.

Frances Ridley Havergal

Beautiful Feet

How beautiful on the mountains
     are the feet of those who bring good news,
who proclaim peace,
     who bring good tidings,
     who proclaim salvation,
who say to Zion,
     "Your God reigns!"

ISAIAH 52:7

Stand firm then, with the belt of truth buckled around
your waist, with the breastplate of righteousness in place,
and with your feet fitted with the readiness that comes
from the gospel of peace.

EPHESIANS 6:14–15

Your word is a lamp to my feet
     and a light for my path.

PSALM 119:105

The Spirit of the Sovereign LORD is on me,
     because the LORD has anointed me
     to preach good news to the poor.
He has sent me to bind up the brokenhearted,
     to proclaim freedom for the captives
     and release from darkness for the prisoners.

ISAIAH 61:1

Shining Sentinels

Driving north from Santa Barbara along the coastal highway, I watched the last bright sliver of sun disappear into the Pacific. My class had run overtime, and I'd stopped for gas, so it was later than I'd planned when I finally headed home.

Too soon gray twilight turned to moonless night, and I crept along, searching the darkness for familiar landmarks. This part of Highway 101 was lovely by day, with the ocean on one side and the mountains on the other, but I didn't like driving it at night. My fingers tightened on the steering wheel as I strained to see where the edge of the road met the shoulder. *No use.* I would have to concentrate on as much of the pavement straight ahead as I could see.

I breathed a prayer. "Lord, please keep me on the road."

As I rounded a curve, my headlights shone on an even row of tiny lights down the middle of the highway. *Like little sentinels!* I thought. *All I have to do is follow them home.*

Those wonderful little reflectors on our nation's highways make me think of the guides God provides for me in my Christian walk. Like the reflectors on the road, my fellow believers and I have no light source on our own. But like Moses, those who turn their hearts toward the Giver of all light reflect his glory, shining along life's pathway. How many times I have reached out to my Christian sister or brother for guidance when I have felt lost or for courage when afraid.

As the highway engineers designed the reflectors for our safety and comfort in driving, our Lord provides us for one another as we travel the paths he has laid for us.

Thank you, Lord, for those who reflect your glory and light the darkness as I travel through life.[42]

Carolyn Johnson

Shining Sentinels

———

[Jesus said,] "Let your light shine before men, that they may see your good deeds and praise your Father in heaven."

MATTHEW 5:16

Those who are wise will shine like the brightness of the heavens, and those who lead many to righteousness, like the stars for ever and ever.

DANIEL 12:3

The path of the righteous is like the first gleam of dawn, shining ever brighter till the full light of day.

PROVERBS 4:18

The light of the righteous shines brightly.

PROVERBS 13:9

[Jesus said,] "The righteous will shine like the sun in the kingdom of their Father."

MATTHEW 13:43

A Witness to the Light

Perhaps you are very dissatisfied with yourself. You are not a genius, have no distinctive gifts, and are inconspicuous when it comes to having any special abilities. Mediocrity seems to be the measure of your existence. None of your days are noteworthy, except for their sameness and lack of zest. Yet in spite of this you may live a great life.

John the Baptist never performed a miracle, but Jesus said of him, "Among those born of women there is no one greater" (Luke 7:28). His mission was to be "a witness to the light" (John 1:8), and that may be your mission and mine. John was content to be only a voice, if it caused people to think of Christ.

Be willing to be only a voice that is heard but not seen, or a mirror whose glass the eye cannot see because it is reflecting the brilliant glory of the Son. Be willing to be a breeze that arises just before daylight, saying, "The dawn! The dawn!" and then fades away.

Do the most everyday and insignificant tasks knowing that God can see. If you live with difficult people, win them over through love. If you once made a great mistake in life, do not allow it to cloud the rest of your life, but by locking it secretly in your heart, make it yield strength and character.

We are doing more good than we know. The things we do today—sowing seeds or sharing simple truths of Christ—people will someday refer to as the first things that prompted them to think of him. For my part, I will be satisfied not to have some great tombstone over my grave but just to know that common people will gather there once I am gone and say, "He was a good man. He never performed any miracles, but he told me about Christ, which led me to know him for myself."[43]

From *Streams in the Desert*

MEDITATIONS ON

a Witness to the Light

My mouth will tell of your righteousness,
of your salvation all day long,
though I know not its measure.
I will come and proclaim your mighty acts,
O Sovereign LORD;
I will proclaim your righteousness, yours alone.
Since my youth, O God, you have taught me,
and to this day I declare your marvelous deeds.

PSALM 71:15–17

[Jesus said,] "You will receive power when the Holy Spirit
comes on you; and you will be my witnesses in Jerusalem,
and in all Judea and Samaria, and to the ends of the earth."

ACTS 1:8

[Jesus said,] "You will be brought before kings and
governors, and all on account of my name. This will
result in your being witnesses to them. But make up
your mind not to worry beforehand how you will defend
yourselves. For I will give you words and wisdom
that none of your adversaries will be able to resist or
contradict."

LUKE 21:12–15

I will praise you, O LORD, with all my heart;
I will tell of all your wonders.

PSALM 9:1

A Time to Heal

"Just picture this," I said to my husband as we surveyed our new backyard. "All of those beautiful rose bushes you've given me for my birthdays would go great over there. And we finally have enough room to have a playhouse for Megan. Now I don't expect anything fancy, but wouldn't it be great to place a small hot tub right here at the end of the grass? Seems to me everyone's needs and wants will be satisfied, and we won't be overextending our budget!" I was sure my suggestions were quite good and felt rather smug as I waited for Matt's response.

One look at his face and my heart sank. He told me that a local veterinarian, who had been rehabilitating hawks and owls for the last 16 years, was turning his attention to other aspects of his profession. "If someone doesn't volunteer to help rehabilitate these birds, local wildlife authorities will be forced to put down even those who have an excellent chance of survival."

That was months ago. Our backyard now has a nice lawn. But large bird cages loom in those places I had envisioned a playhouse and hot tub. Because of my bighearted biologist husband, I have witnessed the healing of many of God's most beautiful creatures. I've also experienced amazing encounters with total strangers who have entered our home, tenderly carrying an array of boxes and blankets housing sick and injured adoptees. Conversations never stay on the birds alone, and I praise God that we've had the opportunity to offer healing words to bird lovers sometimes in great need of encouragement and praise themselves.

Father, thank you for showing me that there really is a time for everything, and that by killing off the trivial you produce significant healing.[44]

Joan Bay Klope

a Time to Heal

There is a time for everything,
and a season for every activity under heaven:
a time to be born and a time to die,
a time to plant and a time to uproot,
a time to kill and a time to heal.

ECCLESIASTES 3:1–3

Encourage one another and build each other up,
just as in fact you are doing.

1 THESSALONIANS 5:11

The tongue that brings healing is a tree of life.

PROVERBS 15:4

Encourage the timid, help the weak, be patient
with everyone.

1 THESSALONIANS 5:14

God is not unjust; he will not forget your work and the
love you have shown him as you have helped his people
and continue to help them.

HEBREWS 6:10

LOVING YOUR NEIGHBOR

M y doorbell rang for the third time that
morning. The urge to ignore it was over-
powering. Instead, I yanked open the door and
looked at my neighbor standing there with a
measuring cup in her hand.

"Can I borrow a cup of sugar?" she asked.

With a forced smile I took her cup,
stomped off to my kitchen and clanked the cup
down on the counter. Mounds of sorted laundry
in front of the washer, breakfast dishes in the
sink, the vacuum cleaner in the middle of the living room floor all filled me with an urgency to
get my housework done. And to top it off, I had
a meeting at the church in just a short time.

But I knew my neighbor was lonely and the
borrowed sugar was only an excuse to visit.
When I turned to hand her the sugar, I saw her
looking at the pictures and plaques on my
kitchen wall. Her eyes flitted from "Friends are
always welcome," which hung over my door, to
"Love one another," above my sink.

In an instant I saw my behavior through her eyes. When had I become so busy that I allowed plaques and pictures to tell about God's love, instead of showing it myself? What was the use of doing church work if I ignored the lonely friends and neighbors around me?

I pulled out a chair for my neighbor and put the tea kettle on the stove. Then I asked her, "What's the rush?"

Lord God, thank you for opportunities to show your love to others. I never want to be too busy to care about those people you put in my life.[45]

Beverly Hamilton

Loving Your Neighbor

———

An expert in the law tested [Jesus] with this question:
"Teacher, which is the greatest commandment in the Law?"
Jesus replied: "'Love the Lord your God with all your
heart and with all your soul and with all your mind.'
This is the first and greatest commandment. And the
second is like it: 'Love your neighbor as yourself.'"

MATTHEW 22:35–39

Each of us should please his neighbor for his good,
to build him up.

ROMANS 15:2

If you really keep the royal law found in Scripture,
"Love your neighbor as yourself," you are doing right.

JAMES 2:8

Dear children, let us not love with words or tongue but
with actions and in truth. This then is how we know
that we belong to the truth.

1 JOHN 3:18–19

NOTHING TO OFFER—
BUT YOURSELF

When I made the commitment to marry a preacher, it was with joy, excitement, and the dream of serving God with all my heart. Up to that point, I had experienced good health, success, achievement, praise, and gratitude. I had every reason to expect that a life of ministry would mean more of the same—plus greater joy and usefulness. I was not prepared for serious and debilitating illness, the miscarriage of a baby, the trauma of a financially troubled church, and personal attacks from the family of faith.

Within one of my husband's sermons, I found a nugget of hope: "Our adversities are God's universities." The adversities drove me to God, and God had what I needed to endure and fulfill the commitment I had made.

In Ruth 1:16–17 the innocent young widow Ruth expresses her passionate and devoted love for her old and bitter mother-in-law. It was not Naomi's beauty, wealth, or even joyfulness that drew Ruth to her, for all of these had long since fallen away.

Rather it was Naomi's faith in the living God, her spiritual wisdom, and her consistent piety that bound the young pagan widow to her.

Ruth made a commitment to travel, live, and pursue life with Naomi, to accept her God and even to die and be buried in Naomi's homeland. Her commitment was not just with loving words and well-meaning feelings, as her sister-in-law Orpah (Ruth 1:14), but with purposeful love and devoted deeds.

Commitment must be fueled not merely by head knowledge but also by heart determination. Ruth had nothing to offer to Naomi or to God but herself, and that she gave willingly and eagerly. Every woman, whatever her circumstances or position, has at least that to give the Savior, and it is enough![46]

Dorothy Patterson

Nothing to Offer
—But Yourself

[Ruth said to Naomi], "Don't urge me to leave you or to turn back from you. Where you go I will go, and where you stay I will stay. Your people will be my people and your God my God. Where you die I will die, and there I will be buried. May the LORD deal with me, be it ever so severely, if anything but death separates you and me."

RUTH 1:16–17

You do not delight in sacrifice, or I would bring it;
*   you do not take pleasure in burnt offerings.*
The sacrifices of God are a broken spirit;
*   a broken and contrite heart,*
*   O God, you will not despise.*

PSALM 51:16–17

To love him with all your heart, with all your understanding and with all your strength, and to love your neighbor as yourself is more important than all burnt offerings and sacrifices.

MARK 12:33

I urge you ... in view of God's mercy, to offer your bodies as living sacrifices, holy and pleasing to God—this is your spiritual act of worship.

ROMANS 12:1

LITTLE IS MUCH

Do I want to do some great thing for God? Perhaps I feel a touch of envy for missionaries or pastors or great leaders and speakers. Perhaps I feel that because what I am doing does not seem as significant, I am not as pleasing to God.

But service for God cannot be evaluated by comparison to other people. The important thing to God is not how I measure up with others, but how I am doing with what he has given me. In the parable of the talents (Matthew 25:14–30), each person was given an amount of money "according to his ability." The man who was given five talents earned five more; the one who received two talents earned two more; but the man who received one talent buried it, refusing to make use of it in any way. The master condemned this man, not because he did not measure up to the others, but because he did not use what he had been given.

God does not see things as we do. He knows what our capabilities are and how he can best use us. If he asks me to be a caring servant to someone and I obey, that is just the same to him as if he had called me to have a worldwide ministry and I obeyed.

I must not wait for some great opportunity in the future to serve him. Whatever he has given me now I must be willing to use, however insignificant it may appear.[47]

June Gunden

Little is much when God is in it!
Labor not for wealth or fame.
There's a crown—and you can win it,
If you go in Jesus' Name.

Does the place you're called to labor
Seem too small and little known?
It is great if God is in it,
And He'll not forget His own.

Kittle L. Suffield

Little Is Much

—————

[Jesus said,] "If you have faith as small as a mustard seed, you can say to this mountain, 'Move from here to there' and it will move. Nothing will be impossible for you."

MATTHEW 17:20

Jesus said, "Whoever can be trusted with very little can also be trusted with much."

LUKE 16:10

Jesus sat down opposite the place where the offerings were put and watched the crowd putting their money into the temple treasury. Many rich people threw in large amounts. But a poor widow came and put in two very small copper coins, worth only a fraction of a penny. Calling his disciples to him, Jesus said, "I tell you the truth, this poor widow has put more into the treasury than all the others. They all gave out of their wealth; but she, out of her poverty, put in everything—all she had to live on."

MARK 12:41–44

"Well done, good and faithful servant! You have been faithful with a few things; I will put you in charge of many things. Come and share your master's happiness!"

MATTHEW 25:21

BLESSINGS FROM ASHES

From top to bottom, our society is success oriented, however one may define that in terms of one's own goals. Christians are not immune; "Everything comes out okay for Christians," and "The King's kids are always winners" are misleading slogans to live by. We develop unrealistic expectations of the Christian life and of ourselves; and then when our wings get broken, we think failure ends our usefulness.

For those of us who know too well the salt taste of failure, it helps to remember that even the great ones of the faith failed, yet God continued to use them, often in a deeper way after their fall.

Some of David's greatest psalms came after his greatest mistakes. God called him "a man after his own heart" (1 Samuel 13:14). Abraham lied, perhaps to save his skin, yet he is the towering example of faith for three major religions and is called "God's friend" (James 2:23).

It is those who have plumbed the depths of failure to whom God invariably gives the call to shepherd others. This is not a call given only to the gifted, the highly trained, or the polished as such.

Without a bitter experience of their own inadequacy and poverty, they are quite unfitted to bear the burden of spiritual ministry. It takes a person who has discovered something of the measure of his own weakness to be patient with the foibles of others. ...

Too many sincere Christians, facing their failures, berate themselves unmercifully and keep asking God for forgiveness. Each of us should memorize, hang on the mirror, and make forever our own the ringing truth: "There is now no [repeat *no*] condemnation for those who are in Christ Jesus" (Romans 8:1).

Not only does he not condemn us; he even brings blessings from the ashes of our failures.[48]

Gini Andrews

Blessings from Ashes

[The Lord has sent me]
to bestow on them a crown of beauty
    instead of ashes,
the oil of gladness
    instead of mourning,
and a garment of praise
    instead of a spirit of despair.
They will be called oaks of righteousness,
    a planting of the LORD
    for the display of his splendor.

ISAIAH 61:3

I Hide your face from my sins
    and blot out all my iniquity.
Create in me a pure heart, O God,
    and renew a steadfast spirit within me.
Do not cast me from your presence
    or take your Holy Spirit from me.
Restore to me the joy of your salvation
    and grant me a willing spirit, to sustain me.
Then I will teach transgressors your ways,
    and sinners will turn back to you.

PSALM 51:9–13

SOWING IN TEARS—
REAPING IN JOY

So often it is assumed that someone who is
going through difficult times is incapable of
effectively ministering to someone else. Indeed,
as we are counseling those who are depressed
and struggling with personal problems, it never
seems to occur to us to encourage them to reach
out to minister to others rather than focus
exclusively on themselves. How insightful the
psalmist was in writing:

He who goes out weeping,
  carrying seed to sow,
will return with songs of joy,
  carrying sheaves with him (Psalm 126:6).

It was during a very stressful period in my
own life a few years ago that I was thrust suddenly into a care-giving situation. I had
promised a friend that I would be a "daughter"
to her mother while she and her husband ful-
filled a two-year mission commitment in Africa.
I might have had second thoughts about my new
role had I realized that the day after my friend
would leave, her mother would enter the hospital where her condition would utterly bewilder
the doctors until she died several weeks later.

I was in no condition to minister to someone else—so I thought. But as I began making those daily hospital visits to Clara, I discovered that instead of adding to my stress, my time with her was rejuvenating. As I identified with her needs, my own problems paled into insignificance. And as I served her and focused on her well-being, I felt better about myself. Clara certainly was not passive in the care-giving process. She responded to my love and gave back to me far more than I gave her. She helped me make it through a very tough time in my life, and I will always have the sweet memories of being close to her during her final days, when I went out weeping and returned with songs of joy.[49]

Ruth A. Tucker

Sowing in Tears and Reaping in Joy

———

Those who sow in tears
will reap with songs of joy.

PSALM 126:5

[Jesus said,] "I tell you the truth, you will weep
and mourn while the world rejoices. You will grieve,
but your grief will turn to joy."

JOHN 16:20

No discipline seems pleasant at the time, but painful.
Later on, however, it produces a harvest of righteousness
and peace for those who have been trained by it.

HEBREWS 12:11

Praise be to the God and Father of our Lord Jesus
Christ, the Father of compassion and the God of all com-
fort, who comforts us in all our troubles, so that we can
comfort those in any trouble with the comfort we our-
selves have received from God.

2 CORINTHIANS 1:3–4

MEETING NEEDS WITH
GENTLE HANDS

Friendship gives license to show up at the door of need without asking, "When would you like me to come?" or "What would you like me to do?" Nor does friendship call out, "Just let me know if you need anything."

Practiced friendship whispers, "I'll be there," and promptly steps through the door with sensitivity, respect, and understanding.

But what about honoring the right to invite? Those who wait for parchment invitations wait long, for need rarely throws a party—rarely even has a voice.

Yet need has its own needs. It needs protection from strangers tromping in with work boots and good intentions. And it needs relief from acquaintances wearing the spiked heels of advice and pat answers.

Need waits with longing for the familiar entrance of dear ones who pad barefoot through the soul on ordinary days.[50]

Susan L. Lenzkes

Do you know the world is dying
For a little bit of love?
Everywhere we hear the sighing
For a little bit of love;
For the love that rights a wrong,
Fills the heart with hope and song;
They have waited, oh, so long,
For a little bit of love.
For a little bit of love,
For a little bit of love,
They have waited, oh, so long,
For a little bit of love,

From the poor of every city,
For a little bit of love,
Hands are reaching out for pity,
For a little bit of love;
Some have burdens hard to bear,
Some have sorrows we would share;
Shall they falter and despair
For a little bit of love?
For a little bit of love,
For a little bit of love,
Shall they falter and despair
For a little bit of love?

Edwin O. Excell

Meeting Needs with Gentle Hands

---

*As God's chosen people, holy and dearly loved,
clothe yourselves with compassion, kindness, humility,
gentleness and patience.*

COLOSSIANS 3:12

*If you spend yourselves in behalf of the hungry
and satisfy the needs of the oppressed,
then your light will rise in the darkness,
and your night will become like the noonday.*

ISAIAH 58:10

*Two are better than one,
because they have a good return for their work:
If one falls down,
his friend can help him up.
But pity the man who falls
and has no one to help him up!*

ECCLESIASTES 4:9–10

Let your gentleness be evident to all. The Lord is near.

PHILIPPIANS 4:5

BE A BRIGHT BLOOM

Dandelions! No matter how carefully I try to pull one up, I never get the whole thing. The root stays deep in the ground, threatening to grow up and blossom again.

But despite their bad reputation, dandelions are pretty little flowers with their yellow strands all tucked neatly into the center. And truly they are the most beautiful of all flowers when presented clutched in a child's dirty little hand. No one gets yelled at for picking them. Perhaps they grow only to be used and enjoyed by children.

Dandelions are ignored or attacked, never nurtured or cared for, and yet they always bloom profusely. They demand no pampering or special attention to yield their bright blossoms; they pop up in fields, in lawns, and between cracks in the sidewalk, even in the best neighborhoods. Can you imagine trying to grow them in a garden? They'd sneak through the boundaries and pop their sunny yellow faces up in the surrounding lawn. They would never stay put!

Christians should be more like dandelions. Our sunny yellow faces should be a reminder that simple faith has deep roots that are impossible to dislodge. Our vast number would show the world that even though we are not fancy or pampered, we are evident everywhere, even in the best neighborhoods.

We should be as easily accessible as a dandelion. Jesus was. We need to get out of our gardens and jump across the boundaries that keep us where people expect to find us. We need to show our sunny yellow faces in all the spots that need a little brightening up—the crack in the sidewalk or the lawn of a country club.[51]

Janice Kempe

Being a Bright Bloom

---

*We, who with unveiled faces all reflect the Lord's glory,
are being transformed into his likeness with
ever-increasing glory, which comes from the Lord,
who is the Spirit.*

2 CORINTHIANS 3:18

*Sing to the LORD, praise his name;
    proclaim his salvation day after day.
Declare his glory among the nations,
    his marvelous deeds among all peoples.*

PSALM 96:2–3

*You turned my wailing into dancing;
    you removed my sackcloth and clothed me with joy,
that my heart may sing to you and not be silent.
    O LORD my God, I will give you thanks forever.*

PSALM 30:11–12

We constantly pray for you, that our God may count you worthy of his calling, and that by his power he may fulfill every good purpose of yours and every act prompted by your faith. We pray this so that the name of our Lord Jesus may be glorified in you, and you in him, according to the grace of our God and the Lord Jesus Christ.

2 THESSALONIANS 1:11–12

Lord, speak to me, that I may speak
In living echoes of thy tone;
As thou hast sought, so let me seek
Thy erring children lost and lone.

O teach me, Lord, that I may teach
The precious things thou dost impart;
And wing my words, that they may reach
The hidden depths of many a heart.

O fill me with thy fullness, Lord,
Until my very heart o'erflow
In kindling thought and glowing word,
Thy love to tell, thy praise to show.

O use me, Lord, use even me,
Just as thou wilt, and when and where;
Until thy blessed face I see,
Thy rest, thy joy, thy glory share.[52]

Frances Ridley Havergal

Healing
OF HEAVEN

TRANQUILITY IN THE HOPE
OF ETERNAL LIFE

A Better World

This world seems solid enough. Whether we ponder the Himalayas or the Grand Canyon, the Pacific Ocean or the polar ice caps, this old earth looks like it's built to last. And it is ... to a point. It will remain until the day that "the heavens will disappear with a roar; the elements will be destroyed by fire, and the earth and everything in it will be laid bare" (2 Peter 3:10). Isaiah gives us a more poetic spin to the same event:

> *"The earth is broken up, ...*
> *the earth is thoroughly shaken.*
> *The earth reels like a drunkard,*
> *it sways like a hut in the wind"*
> (Isaiah 24:19).

Our world may seem eternal, but it's not. Its permanence is an illusion. There is a world, however, whose foundations cannot be shaken and whose streets can never be defiled. Heaven is a real place, and we're going there! It will last as long as its Architect and Maker does, and since God is eternal, so is heaven. Heaven is the place where we will live with Christ forever. And nothing is more solid than that.[53]

Dave and Jan Dravecky

There is a better world, they say
O so bright! O so bright!
Where sin and woe are done away,
O so bright! O so bright!
And music fills the balmy air,
And angels with bright wings are there,
And harps of gold and mansions fair,
O so bright! O so bright!

No clouds e'er pass along that sky,
Happy land! Happy land!
No tear drops glisten in the eye,
Happy land! Happy land!
They drink the gushing streams of grace,
And gaze upon the Savior's face
Whose brightness fills the holy place;
Happy land! Happy land!

John Lyth

MEDITATIONS ON

a Better World

———

We fix our eyes not on what is seen, but on
what is unseen. For what is seen is temporary,
but what is unseen is eternal.

2 CORINTHIANS 4:18

In keeping with [God's] promise we are looking
forward to a new heaven and a new earth,
the home of righteousness.

2 PETER 3:13

I saw a new heaven and a new earth, for the first heaven
and the first earth had passed away, and there was no
longer any sea. I saw the Holy City, the new Jerusalem,
coming down out of heaven from God, prepared as a
bride beautifully dressed for her husband.

REVELATION 21:1–2

"Behold, I will create
    new heavens and a new earth.
The former things will not be remembered,
    nor will they come to mind," [says the LORD.]

ISAIAH 65:17

WE WILL UNDERSTAND

I n spite of our poor choices and spiritual
blindness in this life, our courteous Lord
continues to love us. We will bring him the most
pleasure if we rejoice with him and in him.

When the end comes and we are taken for
judgment above, we will then clearly understand
in God the mysteries that puzzle us now. Not
one of us will think to say, "Lord, if it had been
some other way, all would be well."

We shall all say in unison, "Lord, bless you
because it is all the way it is. It is well. Now we
can honestly see that everything is done as you
intended; you planned it before anything was
ever made."

What is the meaning of it all? Listen carefully. Love is the Lord's meaning. Who reveals it?
Love. Why does he reveal it? For love.

This is the only lesson there is. You will
never learn another. Never. We began in love,
and we shall see all of this in God forever.[54]

Julian of Norwich

I love and love not: Lord, it breaks my heart
    To love and not to love.
Thou veiled within thy glory, gone apart
    Into thy shrine which is above,
Dost thou not love me, Lord, or care
    For this mine ill?—
I love thee here or there
    I will accept thy broken heart, lie still.

Lord, it was well with me in time gone by
    That cometh not again,
When I was fresh and cheerful, who but I?
    I fresh, I cheerful: worn with pain
Now out of sight and out of heart;
    O Lord, how long?—
I watch thee as thou art,
    I will accept thy fainting heart, be strong.

'Lie still,' 'be strong,' today: but Lord, tomorrow,
    What of tomorrow, Lord?
Shall there be rest from toil, be truce from sorrow,
    Be living green upon the sward
Now but a barren grave to me,
    Be joy for sorrow?—
Did I not die for thee?
    Do I not live for thee? Leave Me tomorrow. [55]

Christina Rossetti

We Will Understand

Now we see but a poor reflection as in a mirror;
then we shall see face to face. Now I know in part;
then I shall know fully, even as I am fully known.

1 CORINTHIANS 13:12

My purpose is that they may be encouraged in heart
and united in love, so that they may have the full riches
of complete understanding, in order that they may know
the mystery of God, namely, Christ, in whom are hidden
all the treasures of wisdom and knowledge.

COLOSSIANS 2:2–3

A voice of one calling:
"In the desert prepare
 the way for the LORD;
make straight in the wilderness
 a highway for our God.
Every valley shall be raised up,
 every mountain and hill made low;
the rough ground shall become level,
 the rugged places a plain.
And the glory of the LORD will be revealed,
 and all mankind together will see it.
For the mouth of the LORD has spoken."

ISAIAH 40:3–5

A New Creation

It had been a long night. My sister, Ladonna, was dying, and we who loved her so dearly couldn't stop it. But how we had tried. We had trusted God. We had prayed—I had even fasted and prayed.

We had taken Ladonna to the best cancer specialists and had changed her diet drastically. We cared for her lovingly and tenderly, day and night. We fed her, bathed her, read and sang to her, rubbed her feet and back, and plumped her pillows. We told her jokes and laughed with her—and we hid our eyes so she couldn't see the tears.

Ladonna, too, trusted and prayed. Yet this was to be her final night. She was dying. My other sister, Ruth, held her hand and told her, "Honey, we'll never forget you. We'll see you in every sunrise and in every sunset, in every tree and in every flower."

Looking up at Ruth, Ladonna whispered, ever so softly, "And don't forget the butterflies, Ruthie."

The butterfly—symbol of rebirth and resurrection—what a wonderful reminder! God was freeing Ladonna from pain and heartache. He would resurrect her into a glorious new body, a glorious new life. And she wanted us to remember that.

O God, thank you that someday the heartaches of this world will be left behind. Thanks, too, for the reminder that because I believe in Jesus, I, too, will one day join in your resurrection—in my glorious new body and new life. Amen. [56]

Wilma Brown Giesser

A New Creation

When you sow, you do not plant the body that will be,
but just a seed, perhaps of wheat or of something else.
But God gives it a body as he has determined, and to each
kind of seed he gives its own body. All flesh is not the
same: Men have one kind of flesh, animals have another,
birds another and fish another. There are also heavenly
bodies and there are earthly bodies; but the splendor of
the heavenly bodies is one kind, and the splendor of the
earthly bodies is another. The sun has one kind of splendor,
the moon another and the stars another; and star differs
from star in splendor.

So will it be with the resurrection of the dead. The
body that is sown is perishable, it is raised imperishable;
it is sown in dishonor, it is raised in glory; it is sown in
weakness, it is raised in power.

1 CORINTHIANS 15:37–43

Our citizenship is in heaven. And we eagerly await a
Savior from there, the Lord Jesus Christ, who, by the
power that enables him to bring everything under his
control, will transform our lowly bodies so that they
will be like his glorious body.

PHILIPPIANS 3:20–21

WAITING FOR HOPE

There are times when everything looks very dark to me—so dark that I have to wait before I have hope. Waiting *with* hope is very difficult, but true patience is expressed when we must even wait *for* hope. When we see no hint of success yet refuse to despair, when we see nothing but darkness of night through our window yet keep the shutters open because stars may appear in the sky, and when we have an empty place in our heart yet will not allow it to be filled with anything less than God's best—that is the greatest kind of patience in the universe. It is the story of Job in the midst of the storm, Abraham on the road to Moriah, Moses in the desert of Midian, and the Son of Man in the Garden of Gethsemane. And there is no patience as strong as that which endures because we see "him who is invisible" (Hebrews 11:27). It is the kind of patience that waits for hope.

Dear Lord, you have made waiting beautiful and patience divine. You have taught us that your will should be accepted simply because it *is* your will.

You have revealed to us that a person may see nothing but sorrow in his cup yet still be willing to drink it because of a conviction that your eyes see further than his own.

Father, give me your divine power—the power of Gethsemane. Give me the strength to wait for hope—to look through the window when there are no stars. Even when my joy is gone, give me the strength to stand victoriously in the darkest night and say, "To my heavenly Father, the sun still shines."

I will have reached the point of greatest strength once I have learned to wait for hope.

Strive to be one of the few who walk this earth with the ever present realization—every morning, noon, and night—that the unknown that people call heaven is directly behind those things that are visible.[57]

From *Streams in the Desert*

Waiting for Hope

———

Faith is being sure of what we hope for and certain of what we do not see.

HEBREWS 11:1

Christ is faithful as a son over God's house. And we are his house, if we hold on to our courage and the hope of which we boast.

HEBREWS 3:6

The grace of God that brings salvation has appeared to all men. It teaches us to say "No" to ungodliness and worldly passions, and to live self-controlled, upright and godly lives in this present age, while we wait for the blessed hope—the glorious appearing of our great God and Savior, Jesus Christ.

TITUS 2:11–13

Find rest, O my soul, in God alone;
my hope comes from him.

PSALM 62:5

Always Enough

The greatest lesson a soul has to learn is that God, and God alone, is enough for all his needs. This is a lesson that all God's dealings with us are meant to teach, and this is the crowning discovery of our entire Christian life. GOD IS ENOUGH!

No soul can really be at rest until it has given up dependence on everything else and has been forced to depend on the Lord alone. As long as our expectation is from other things, nothing but disappointment awaits us. Feelings may change, doctrines and dogmas may be upset, the Christian work may come to naught, prayers may seem to lose their fervency, promises may seem to fail, everything that we have believed in or depended on may seem to be swept away, and only God is left—just God, the bare God if I may be allowed the expression, simply and only God.

If God is what he would seem to be from his revealings; if he is indeed the "God of all comfort" (2 Corinthians 1:3); if he is our shepherd; if he is really and truly our Father; if, in short, all the many aspects he has told us of his character and his ways are actually true, then we must come to the positive conviction that he is, in himself alone, enough for all our needs and that we may safely rest in him absolutely and forever.[58]

Hannah Whitall Smith

Always enough of grace is giv'n to me from day to day,
Always enough of grace to help me on the upward way.

Always enough of comfort to console me when I'm sad,
Always enough of peace in time of storm to make me glad.

Always enough of Jesus' love to fill me with delight,
Always enough of hope to keep faith's altar burning bright.

Always enough of joy to make my heart rejoice and sing,
Always enough of pleasure in the service of my King.

Always enough for me, for me,
Always enough for me, for me,
This is my song, the whole day long,
There's always enough for me.

William L. Dale

Always Enough

---

*[Jesus said,] "My grace is sufficient for you,
for my power is made perfect in weakness."*

2 CORINTHIANS 12:9

To me, to live is Christ and to die is gain.

PHILIPPIANS 1:21

*Whatever was to my profit I now consider loss for the
sake of Christ. What is more, I consider everything a
loss compared to the surpassing greatness of knowing
Christ Jesus my Lord, for whose sake I have lost all
things. I consider them rubbish, that I may gain Christ.*

PHILIPPIANS 3:7–8

*I know what it is to be in need, and I know what it is to
have plenty. I have learned the secret of being content in
any and every situation, whether well fed or hungry,
whether living in plenty or in want. I can do everything
through [Christ] who gives me strength.*

PHILIPPIANS 4:12–13

THE JOY OF HEAVEN

Lord, why should I doubt any more when you have given me such assured pledges of your love? First, you are my Creator, I your creature, you my master, I your servant. But from there arises not my comfort, for you are my Father, I your child; "Ye shall be my sons and daughters" (2 Corinthians 6:18 KJV) says the Lord Almighty. Christ is my brother, I ascend to my Father, and your Father, to my God and your God; but lest this should not be enough, my maker is my husband. Even more, I am a member of his body, he my head. Such privileges, had not the Word of truth made them known, who or where is the man that would have thought of it? So wonderful are these thoughts that my spirit fails in me at the consideration of them, and I am confounded to think that God, who has done so much for me, should have so little from me. But this is my comfort, when I come to heaven, I shall understand perfectly what he has done for me, and then shall I be able to praise him as I ought. Lord, having this hope, let me purify myself as you are pure, and let me be no more afraid of death, but even desire to be dissolved and be with you, which is best of all.[59]

Anne Bradstreet

Someday the silver cord will break,
And I no more as now shall sing.
But, oh, the joy when I shall wake
Within the palace of the King!

Someday my earthly house will fall;
I cannot tell how soon 'twill be,
But this I know—my All in All
Has now a place in heav'n for me.

Someday, when fades the golden sun
Beneath the rosy-tinted west,
My blessed Lord will say, "Well done!"
And I shall enter into rest.

Someday, till then I'll watch and wait,
My lamp all trimmed and burning bright,
That when my Savior opens the gate,
My soul to him may take its flight.

And I shall see him face to face,
And tell the story—saved by grace:
And I shall see him face to face,
And tell the story—saved by grace.

Fanny Crosby

MEDITATIONS ON

the Joy of Heaven

———

I heard every creature in heaven and on earth and under
the earth and on the sea, and all that is in them, singing:
"To him who sits on the throne and to the Lamb
be praise and honor and glory and power,
for ever and ever!"

REVELATION 5:13

[Jesus said,] "Rejoice that your names are written
in heaven."

LUKE 10:20

You guide me with your counsel, [LORD,]
and afterward you will take me into glory.
Whom have I in heaven but you?
And earth has nothing I desire besides you.

PSALM 73:24–25

The ransomed of the LORD will return.
They will enter Zion with singing;
everlasting joy will crown their heads.
Gladness and joy will overtake them,
and sorrow and sighing will flee away.

ISAIAH 51:11

HOPE FOR THE HOPELESS

I feel like I could cry forever. I miss him so much that I actually hurt inside. Will my life ever be the same?"

Have you felt the deep sorrow of the mourning widow? If you have lost a child, parent, close relative or friend, perhaps you have also felt comfortless. Is there anyone who can minister to you when you feel overwhelmed with grief?

The psalmist shows that he identifies with the pain of the bereaved:

The cords of death entangled me,
the anguish of the grave came upon me;
I was overcome by trouble and sorrow (Psalm 116:3).

Enveloped by emptiness, loneliness and stress, who does the psalmist turn to?
I called on the name of the LORD:
"O LORD, save me!" (Psalm 116:4)

He turns to the only one who will dry all of our tears (Isaiah 25:8); the one who carries all of our sorrows (Isaiah 53:4); the man acquainted with grief (Isaiah 53:3).

Likewise we must turn to God and his Word for comfort in our times of sorrow. Without denying our pain, Scripture gives us a proper perspective, something we can easily lose in times of emotional trauma and crisis.

God's Word gives hope when we feel utterly alone and hopeless. We can take comfort in knowing that God does not allow a trial in our lives that is too great for us to bear (1 Corinthians 10:13). We can also be assured that death does not conquer those who die in Christ (1 Corinthians 15:22, 53–56).

God is in charge of all things. Even the terrible destruction and the traumatic aftermath of death for those who mourn are under his lordship. God's Word and Spirit can comfort our grieving hearts so that we will be able to say with the psalmist:

I may walk before the LORD
*   in the land of the living ...*
I am [his] servant....
Praise the LORD (Psalm 116:9, 16, 19).[60]

Carol L. Baldwin

Hope for the Hopeless

[The LORD Almighty] will swallow up death forever.
The Sovereign LORD will wipe away the tears
  from all faces;
he will remove the disgrace of his people
  from all the earth.
The LORD has spoken.

ISAIAH 25:8

He was despised and rejected by men,
  a man of sorrows, and familiar with suffering.

ISAIAH 53:3

The perishable must clothe itself with the imperishable,
and the mortal with immortality. When the perishable
has been clothed with the imperishable, and the mortal
with immortality, then the saying that is written will
come true: "Death has been swallowed up in victory."

  "Where, O death, is your victory?
    Where, O death, is your sting?"

1 CORINTHIANS 15:53–55

EVERLASTING LOVE

I n church school I learned that Jesus loved us. I've believed it all my life. As an adult I became the teacher who taught God's love in church school classes, Bible studies, churches, and conferences around the world. I thought I really understood how much God cares for us. But then tragedy hit. I was forced to reach into the spiritual well within me, and I came up lacking. I asked the Lord why good people suffer. Night and day I prayed, pleading with God to either perform a tangible miracle or change my heart and remove the pain. I felt abandoned.

Then I decided I simply must discover the magnitude of God's love and learn to know him on a deeper spiritual level. I couldn't depend on circumstances for proof of his love and approval. Even though I had been through trials before, I still needed to learn that his love transcends both good and bad circumstances. That is when he spoke clearly to me through Jeremiah 31:3:

> *I have loved you with an everlasting love;*
> *I have drawn you with loving-kindness.*

The words struck me hard, like bolts of lightning. I was stunned, overwhelmed. It was as though God personally put his loving arms around me and said, "Marie, I don't promise that my children will never suffer in this life, but I assure you that through every experience I'll love you with love that is everlasting. I'll constantly draw you to myself with my loving-kindness in spite of anything you're experiencing."

The magnitude of his love—even through sorrow and tragedy—revolutionized my life. Jeremiah 31:3 became my life verse. I labeled myself a "Loved Person," and I've continued to believe it. Though I've lived through other hardships since that time, I've never lost my awareness of his love for me.

God wants us to participate in this love relationship because it is the foundation of life. This love is everlasting. Unchanging. Forever. We can each consider ourselves a Loved Person, not because of our circumstances or situations but simply because God loves us perfectly, totally, and eternally.[61]

Marie Chapian

Everlasting Love

Give thanks to the LORD, for he is good;
his love endures forever.

1 CHRONICLES 16:34

Surely goodness and love will follow me
all the days of my life,
and I will dwell in the house of the LORD forever.

PSALM 23:6

I am like an olive tree
flourishing in the house of God;
I trust in God's unfailing love
for ever and ever.

PSALM 52:8

I will declare that your love stands firm forever,
that you established your faithfulness in heaven
itself.

PSALM 89:2

From everlasting to everlasting
the LORD's love is with those who fear him,
and his righteousness with their children's children.

PSALM 103:17

My New Home

The owner of the house I have lived in for many years has notified me that he will do little or nothing to keep it in repair. He also advised me to be ready to move.

At first this was not very welcome news. In many respects the surrounding area is quite pleasant, and if not for the evidence of a somewhat declining condition, the house seems rather nice. Yet a closer look reveals that even a light wind causes it to shake and sway, and its foundation is not sufficient to make it secure. Therefore I am getting ready to move.

As I consider the move, it is strange how quickly my interest is transferred to my prospective new home in another country. I have been consulting maps and studying accounts of its inhabitants. And someone who has come from there to visit has told me that it is beautiful beyond description and that language is inadequate to fully describe what he heard while there. He said that in order to make an investment there, he has suffered the loss of everything he owned here, yet rejoices in what others would call a sacrifice.

Another person, whose love for me has been proved by the greatest possible test, now lives there. He has sent me several clusters of the most delicious grapes I have ever eaten, and after tasting them everything here tastes very bland.

Several times I have gone to the edge of the river that forms the boundary between here and there and have longed to be with those singing praises to the King on the other side. Many of my friends have moved across that river, but before leaving here they spoke of my following them later. I have seen the smile on their faces as they passed from my sight. So each time I am asked to make some new investment here, I now respond, "I am getting ready to move."[62]

From *Streams in the Desert*

My New Home

——————

All these people [heroes of the faith] were still living by faith when they died. They did not receive the things promised; they only saw them and welcomed them from a distance. And they admitted that they were aliens and strangers on earth. People who say such things show that they are looking for a country of their own. If they had been thinking of the country they had left, they would have had opportunity to return. Instead, they were longing for a better country—a heavenly one. Therefore God is not ashamed to be called their God, for he has prepared a city for them.

HEBREWS 11:13–16

Listen, I tell you a mystery: We will not all sleep, but we will all be changed—in a flash, in the twinkling of an eye, at the last trumpet. For the trumpet will sound, the dead will be raised imperishable, and we will be changed.

1 CORINTHIANS 15:51–52

We know that if the earthly tent we live in is destroyed, we have a building from God, an eternal house in heaven, not built by human hands.

2 CORINTHIANS 5:1

THE ETERNAL
SPRING TO COME

The vernal equinox is that period in the cycle of the seasons in which days and nights are equal in length. Children, who would pipe with Pan in the spirit of eternal spring, will argue that the nights are longer (but winter-weary parents have a rebuttal for that!) Surely everybody throughout the world must love the season when, as Browning put it, "God's in His Heaven—all's right with the world."

Rusty pine needles are dropping and the trees thrust up new green sprays to cover the few that refused to leave the parent tree. I notice there are fat, pink buds on the Thundercloud plum—a sight that never fails to bring a sad-sweet ache of memory. I always loved hearing my father sing the old hymn, "The Unclouded Day." It is one of those decep-tively warm days today, without a cloud to mar the blue; and it takes little imagination to see the flowering plum as "the Tree of Life in Eternal Bloom," shedding its fragrance over a land where life has begun anew. Even the vul-ture, which wheeled over the scene looking for signs of death, has given up and sailed away.

And yet, paradoxically, it was death which brought about this unbelievably brilliant beauty. Each tender shoot of grass beneath my feet sprang from last year's seed. Each daffodil was a dull, brown bulb giving no hint of the ruffled trumpet inside. Now each bloom looks as if it carries the image of the sun itself, caught and cupped in the shining throat. Memory allows me to hear my father's voice a little louder: "Oh, they tell me of a land where no storm clouds rise."

There is such a place; there will be such a day. And we, in his image, shall rise up to meet him—much as the daffodils pattern the sun.[63]

June Masters Bacher

MEDITATIONS ON

the Eternal Spring to Come

———

The angel showed me the river of the water of life,
as clear as crystal, flowing from the throne of God and
of the Lamb down the middle of the great street of the
city. On each side of the river stood the tree of life, bear-
ing twelve crops of fruit, yielding its fruit every month.
And the leaves of the tree are for the healing of the
nations. No longer will there be any curse. The throne
of God and of the Lamb will be in the city, and his
servants will serve him. They will see his face, and his
name will be on their foreheads. There will be no more
night. They will not need the light of a lamp or the light
of the sun, for the Lord God will give them light.
And they will reign for ever and ever.

REVELATION 22:1–5

"I will pour water on the thirsty land,
    and streams on the dry ground;
I will pour out my Spirit on your offspring,
    and my blessing on your descendants.
They will spring up like grass in a meadow,
    like poplar trees by flowing streams," [says the LORD.*]*

ISAIAH 44:3–4

Goodness and Mercy Forever

In David's daily walk with God he learned that his Good Shepherd was sufficient for every need. He could say from his personal experience, "Surely goodness and mercy shall follow me all the days of my life."

As we look ahead we cannot see "all the days of my life" that lie ahead. David said "ALL" the days, January through December; not just the bright days but the dark ones, not only the easy days but the difficult ones. He doesn't say months or years, but "days"—the "days of my life," each one of them.

Do we look ahead and wonder what next year or next week or tomorrow holds for us? Regardless of what comes, there will never be a day that God's choice guardians, goodness and mercy, will not follow us. They will accompany us every day on our earthly pilgrimage.

They are attributes of God. David wrote,

"O taste and see that the Lord is GOOD" (Psalm 34:8 KJV).

Paul wrote, "God, who is rich in mercy" (Ephesians 2:4 KJV).

Someone has said, "Goodness to supply every want, mercy to forgive every sin; goodness to provide, mercy to pardon."

David said, "SURELY goodness and mercy shall follow me." We can be assured of this because he has never failed in the past; because he has pledged his Word and it has never failed. We can have assurance of knowing that his goodness and mercy are with us today.

It is personal for us, as it was for David. We can say, "shall follow ME all the days of MY life."

When life comes to a close on earth, I can say, "I will dwell in the house of the LORD for ever." Jesus promised, "In my Father's house are many mansions: if it were not so, I would have told you. I go to prepare a place for you. And if I go and prepare a place for you, I will come again, and receive you unto myself; that where I am, there ye may be also" (John 14:2–3 KJV).[64]

Millie Stamm

MEDITATIONS ON

Goodness and Mercy Forever

—————

*Because of his great love for us, God, who is rich in
mercy, made us alive with Christ even when we were
dead in transgressions—it is by grace you have been
saved. And God raised us up with Christ and seated
us with him in the heavenly realms in Christ Jesus,
in order that in the coming ages he might show the
incomparable riches of his grace, expressed in his
kindness to us in Christ Jesus.*

EPHESIANS 2:4–7

*How great is your goodness,
    which you [LORD] have stored up for those
    who fear you,
which you bestow in the sight of men
    on those who take refuge in you.*

PSALM 31:19

*In all their distress [the LORD] too was distressed,
    and the angel of his presence saved them.
In his love and mercy he redeemed them;
    he lifted them up and carried them
    all the days of old.*

ISAIAH 63:9

THE GOD OF ALL COMFORT

The reality of being comforted seems to me almost more delightful than any other thing in life. When as little children we have cuddled up into our mother's lap after a fall or a misfortune, and have felt her dear arms around us, and her soft kisses on our hair, we have had comfort. When, as grown-up people, after a hard day's work, we have put on our slippers and seated ourselves by the fire, in an easy chair with a book, we have had comfort. When someone whom we dearly love has been ill almost unto death, and has been restored to us in health again, we have had comfort.

He is the "God, who comforts the downcast" (2 Corinthians 7:6); it is just because you are downcast that you can claim the comforting of Christ. The psalmist tells us that God will "comfort [us] on every side" (Psalm 71:21 KJV), and what an all-embracing bit of comfort this is. "On every side," no aching spot to be left uncomforted.

The "God of all comfort" sent his Son to be the Comforter of a mourning world.

Our Comforter is close at hand. He abides with us. He declared, "Peace I leave with you, My peace I give to you; not as the world gives do I give to you. Let not your heart be troubled, neither let it be afraid" (John 14:27 NKJV).

How can we, in the face of these tender and loving words, go about with troubled and frightened hearts? God's comfort is being continually and abundantly given, but unless you will accept it you cannot have it. In this matter of comfort it is exactly as it is in every other experience in the religious life. God says, "Believe, and then you can feel."

If we want to be comforted, we must make up our minds to believe every word of comfort God has ever spoken; and we must refuse to listen to any words of discomfort spoken by our own hearts or our circumstances.[65]

Hannah Whitall Smith

the God of All Comfort

———

Your righteousness reaches to the skies, O God,
you who have done great things.
Who, O God, is like you? ...
You will increase my honor
and comfort me once again.

PSALM 71:19, 21

May your unfailing love be my comfort,
according to your promise to your servant.

PSALM 119:76

Shout for joy, O heavens;
rejoice, O earth;
burst into song, O mountains!
For the LORD *comforts his people*
and will have compassion on his afflicted ones.

ISAIAH 49:13

[Jesus said,] "Blessed are those who mourn,
for they will be comforted."

MATTHEW 5:4

UNTIL YOUR JOURNEY
IS THROUGH

"Thus far has the Lord helped us."
1 Samuel 7:12

The words "thus far" are like a hand pointing in the direction of the past. It had been "a long time, twenty years in all" (v. 2), but even if it had been seventy years, "Thus far has the Lord helped"! Whether through poverty, wealth, sickness, or health, whether at home or abroad, or on land, sea, or air, and whether in honor, dishonor, difficulties, joy, trials, triumph, prayer, or temptation—"Thus far has the Lord helped"!

We always enjoy looking down a long road lined with beautiful trees. The trees are a delightful sight and seem to form a temple of plants, with strong wooden pillars and arches of leaves. In the same way you look down a beautiful road like this, why not look back on the road of the years of your life? Look at the large green limbs of God's mercy overhead and the strong pillars of his loving-kindness and faithfulness that have brought you much joy. Do you see any birds singing in the branches? If you look closely, surely you will see many, for they are singing of God's mercy received "thus far."

These words also point forward. Someone who comes to a certain point and writes the words "thus far" realizes that he has not yet come to the end of the road and that he still had some distance to travel. There are still more trials, joys, temptations, battles, defeats, victories, prayers, answers, toils, and strength yet to come. ...

Then is life over after death? No! These are still yet to come: arising in the likeness of Jesus; thrones, harps, and the singing of psalms; being "clothed in white garments" (Revelation 3:5 NASB), seeing the face of Jesus, and sharing fellowship with the saints; and experiencing the glory of God, the fullness of eternity, and infinite joy. So dear believer, "be strong and take heart" (Psalm 27:14), and with thanksgiving and confidence lift your voice in praise for:

The Lord who "thus far" has helped you
Will help you all your journey through.

When the words "thus far" are read in heaven's light, what glorious and miraculous prospects they reveal to our grateful eyes! [66]

From *Streams in the Desert*

Until Your Journey Is Through

———

The LORD himself goes before you and will be with you; he will never leave you nor forsake you. Do not be afraid; do not be discouraged.

DEUTERONOMY 31:8

[Jesus said,] "I will ask the Father, and he will give you another Counselor to be with you forever—the Spirit of truth. ... You know him, for he lives with you and will be in you. I will not leave you as orphans; I will come to you."

JOHN 14:16–18

This is what the LORD says...
"Fear not, for I have redeemed you;
  I have summoned you by name; you are mine.
When you pass through the waters,
  I will be with you;
and when you pass through the rivers,
  they will not sweep over you.
When you walk through the fire,
  you will not be burned;
  the flames will not set you ablaze.

ISAIAH 43:1–2

[Jesus said,] "Surely I am with you always, to the very end of the age."

MATTHEW 28:20

No More Tears

Are you an individual who has difficulty sleeping at night? The harder you try, the more you toss and turn. Sometimes our wakefulness is caused by sorrow, pain, or heartache. During the dark night hours the tears fall. Our hearts may be broken. Loneliness may overwhelm us.

David knew what it was to shed tears. "You have seen me tossing and turning in the night. You have collected all my tears and preserved them in your bottle" (Psalm 56:8 TLB). We read that in Persia and Egypt, tears were sometimes wiped from the eyes and cheeks of the mourner and preserved in a tear bottle. Often a person's tear bottle was buried with him. David asked God to preserve his tears in a bottle and record them in his book.

Sometimes a child will cry over a broken toy. As the parent mends it and returns it to the child, a smile breaks through the tears. Sometimes, however, it is broken beyond repair. Then the parent has to become a special comforter, for the toy will have to be replaced with something else.

Sometimes our tears come from a broken heart. God mends it, and we smile again through our tears. But sometimes God knows that for our own good he must remove something from our lives, something we may consider very dear. The tears may fall; we may not understand why, yet he does it for our good. However, he never removes anything from our lives without replacing it with something else. It has been said, "Our broken things lead us to his better things." God comforts as no one else does. He understands as no one else does.

A time is coming when all tears will be wiped from our eyes. One of these days, we will go to live with him eternally. "And God shall wipe away ALL tears from their eyes; and there shall be no more death, neither sorrow, nor crying, neither shall there be any more pain: for the former things are passed away" (Revelation 21:4 KJV).[67]

Millie Stamm

MEDITATIONS ON

No More Tears

These are they who have come out of the great tribula-
tion; they have washed their robes and made them white
in the blood of the Lamb.

Therefore,
"they are before the throne of God
and serve him day and night in his temple;
and he who sits on the throne will spread his tent over
them.
Never again will they hunger;
never again will they thirst.
The sun will not beat upon them,
nor any scorching heat.
For the Lamb at the center of the throne will be
their shepherd;
he will lead them to springs of living water.
And God will wipe away every tear from their eyes."

REVELATION 7:14–17

THE OTHER WORLD

It lies around us like a cloud—
    The world we do not see;
Yet the sweet closing of an eye
    May bring us there to be.

Its gentle breezes fan our cheeks
    Amid our worldly cares;
Its gentle voices whisper love,
    And mingle with our prayers.

Sweet hearts around us throb and beat,
    Sweet helping hands are stirred,
And palpitates the veil between
    With breathings almost heard.

The silence—awful, sweet, and calm
    They have no power to break;
For mortal words are not for them
    To utter or partake.

So thin, so soft, so sweet they glide,
    So near to press they seem,
They lull us gently to our rest,
    And melt into our dream.

And, in the hush of rest they bring,
    'Tis easy now to see
How lovely and how sweet a pass
    The hour of death may be!

To close the eye and close the ear,
    Wrapped in a trance of bliss,
And, gently drawn in loving arms,
    To swoon to that—from this.

Scarce knowing if we wake or sleep,
    Scarce asking where we are,
To feel all evil sink away,
    All sorrow and all care.

Sweet souls around us! Watch us still,
    Press nearer to our side,
Into our thoughts, into our prayers,
    With gentle helping glide.

Let death between us be as naught,
    A dried and vanished stream;
Your joy be the reality,
    Our suffering life the dream.

Harriet Beecher Stowe

MEDITATIONS ON

the Other World

I heard a loud voice from the throne saying, "Now the dwelling of God is with men, and he will live with them. They will be his people, and God himself will be with them and be their God. He will wipe every tear from their eyes. There will be no more death or mourning or crying or pain, for the old order of things has passed away."

He who was seated on the throne said, "I am making everything new!" Then he said, "Write this down, for these words are trustworthy and true." . . .

One of the seven angels who had the seven bowls full of the seven last plagues came and said to me, "Come, I will show you the bride, the wife of the Lamb." And he carried me away in the Spirit to a mountain great and high, and showed me the Holy City, Jerusalem, coming down out of heaven from God. It shone with the glory of God, and its brilliance was like that of a very precious jewel, like a jasper, clear as crystal.

REVELATION 21:3–5, 9–11

There's a land that is fairer than day,
And by faith we can see it afar;
For the Father waits over the way
To prepare us a dwelling place there.

In the sweet by and by,
We shall meet on that beautiful shore;
In the sweet by and by,
We shall meet on that beautiful shore.

We shall sing on that beautiful shore
The melodious songs of the blessed;
And our spirits shall sorrow no more,
Not a sigh for the blessing of rest.

In the sweet by and by,
We shall meet on that beautiful shore;
In the sweet by and by,
We shall meet on that beautiful shore.

To our bountiful Father above,
We will offer our tribute of praise
For the glorious gift of His love
And the blessings that hallow our days.

Sanford F. Bennett

NOTES

[1]Millie Stamm, *Beside Still Waters* (Grand Rapids: Zondervan, 1984), 52–3.

[2]Judith Couchman, *Shaping a Woman's Soul* (Grand Rapids: Zondervan, 1996), 18–9.

[3]Hannah Whitall Smith, *Perfect Peace: Selections from the God of All Comfort* (Chicago: Moody, 2000), 70–1.

[4]Couchman, 171–3.

[5]Karen Burton Mains, in Mary Beckwith, compiler, *Still Moments* (Ventura, CA: Regal, 1989), 52.

[6]Smith, 53–4.

[7]Marlene Bagnull, in *Still Moments*, 74–5.

[8]Stamm, 106–7.

[9]Smith, 86–7.

[10]Anna Shipton, in L.B. Cowman, *Streams in the Desert* (Grand Rapids, Zondervan, 1997), March 19.

[11]Frances Ridley Havergal, in *The Classics Devotional Bible* (Grand Rapids, Zondervan, 1996), 929.

[12]Smith, in *The Classics Devotional Bible*, 1073.

[13]*Streams in the Desert*, January 15.

[14]Elizabeth Singer Rowe, in Bernard Bangley, compiler. *Near to the Heart of God* (Wheaton: Harold Shaw, 1998), December 20.

[15]*Streams in the Desert*, January 16.

[16]Stamm, 27–29.

[17]Bagnull, in *Still Moments*, 241–2.

[18]Anne Bradstreet, in *The Classics Devotional Bible*, 595.

[19]Couchman, 23–24.

[20]*Streams in the Desert*, January 30.

[21]Smith, in *The Classics Devotional Bible*, 1467.

[22]Neva B. True, in *Still Moments*, 122–3.

[23]Julian of Norwich, in *Near to the Heart of God*, February 15.

[24]Couchman, 79–80.

[25]Stamm, 16–17.

[26]*Near to the Heart of God*, June 21.

[27]Catherine Parr, in *Near to the Heart of God*, March 13.

[28]Couchman, 104–105.

[29]*Streams in the Desert*, October 26.

[30]Teresa of Avila, in *Near to the Heart of God*, March 28.

[31] Stamm, 82–3.

[32] Beryl Henne, in *Still Moments*, 23–4.

[33] Couchman, 94–6.

[34] Edith Willis Linn, in *Streams in the Desert*, February 15

[35] June Masters Bacher, *Quiet Moments for Women* (Eugene, OR: Harvest House, 1979), October 10.

[36] *Streams in the Desert*, December 4.

[37] Josephine Smith, in *Still Moments*, 25–6.

[38] Bacher, May 3.

[39] Beverly Hamilton, in *Still Moments*, 39–40.

[40] Couchman, 182–4.

[41] Haveral, in *The Classics Devotional Bible*, 1058.

[42] Carolyn Johnson, in *Still Moments*, 37–8.

[43] *Streams in the Desert*, February 24.

[44] Joan Bay Klope, in *Still Moments*, 49–50.

[45] Hamilton, in *Still Moments*, 59–60.

[46] Dorothy Patterson, in *The Women's Devotional Bible I* (Grand Rapids: Zondervan, 1990), 272.

[47] June Gunden, in *The Women's Devotional Bible I*, 383.

[48] Gini Andrews, in *The Women's Devotional Bible I*, 592.

[49] Ruth A. Tucker, in *The Women's Devotional Bible I*, 646.

[50] Susan L. Lenzkes, in *The Women's Devotional Bible I*, 681.

[51] Janice Kempe, in *The Women's Devotional Bible I*, 1067.

[52] Havergal, *The Women's Devotional Bible I*, 778.

[53] Dave and Jan Dravecky, *Do Not Lose Heart* (Grand Rapids: Zondervan, 1998), 137.

[54] Julian of Norwich, in *Near to the Heart of God*, December 29.

[55] Christina Rossetti, in *The Classics Devotional Bible*, 675.

[56] Wilma Brown Giesser, in *Still Moments*, 262.

[57] *Streams in the Desert*, July 26.

[58] Hannah Whitall Smith, in *The Women's Devotional Bible I*, 237.

[59] Anne Bradstreet, in *The Classics Devotional Bible*, 1360.

[60] Carol L. Baldwin, in *The Women's Devotional Bible I*, 638.

[61] Marie Chapian, in *The Women's Devotional Bible I*, 838.

[62] *Streams in the Desert*, October 21.

[63] Bacher, March 21.

[64] Stamm, 34–5.

[65] Smith, *Perfect Peace*, 28–9.

[66] *Streams in the Desert*, December 31.

[67] Stamm, 76–7.

At Inspirio, we love to hear from you
—your stories, your feedback,
and your product ideas.
Please send your comments to us
by way of email at
icares@zondervan.com
or to the address below:

inspirio

Attn: Inspirio Cares
5300 Patterson Avenue SE
Grand Rapids, MI 49530

If you would like further information
about Inspirio and the products we
create please visit us at:
www.inspiriogifts.com

Thank you and God bless!